GONE THE
HARD
ROAD

GONE THE HARD ROAD

A Memoir

—⁓—

LEE MARTIN

INDIANA UNIVERSITY PRESS

This book is a publication of

Indiana University Press
Office of Scholarly Publishing
Herman B Wells Library 350
1320 East 10th Street
Bloomington, Indiana 47405 USA

iupress.org

Manufactured in the United States of America

Library in Congress Cataloging-in-Publication Data

Names: Martin, Lee, 1955- author.
Title: Gone the hard road : a memoir / Lee Martin.
Description: Bloomington, Indiana : Indiana University Press, [2021] | Summary: "Gone the Hard Road is the story of a mother's endurance and sacrifice, and the gift of imagination she gave her son. Extending Lee Martin's acclaimed first memoir, From Our House, which told the story of the farming accident that cost his father both his hands and led to his rage, this new book focuses more on Martin's mother and the world she created for him within their unsettled family life. From the first time she read to him in a doctor's office waiting room, to her enrolling him in a children's book club, to the first time she took him to a public library, to the books she bought him when he was in high school, this narrative portrays the selfless actions she took, sometimes despite her husband's opposition, to show her son a different way of living. Whereas From Our House and Martin's second memoir, Such a Life, concentrated on the life his father threatened to destroy, Gone the Hard Road tells the story of a loving mother and the life she made possible, even though she knew the eventual cost to herself. A poignant, honest, and moving read, Martin's story about leaving home will stay with anyone who has ever struggled to find their place in the world"—Provided by publisher.
Identifiers: LCCN 2020009494 | ISBN 9780253053862 (cloth ; alk. paper) | ISBN 9780253053886 (pdf)
Subjects: LCSH: Martin, Lee, 1955- | Authors, American—20th century—Biography.
Classification: LCC PS3563.A724927 Z46 2021 | DDC 813/.54 [B]—dc23
LC record available at https://lccn.loc.gov/2020009494

1 2 3 4 5 25 24 23 22 21

for Cathy

CONTENTS

GONE THE HARD ROAD

The Hard Road

We called the paved road we traveled from our farm to the tiny town of Sumner, Illinois, the blacktop or the hard road. Our township was made up of gravel roads that ran at right angles in one-mile sections along fields of wheat or soybeans or corn. We drove those roads with pickup trucks, grain trucks, tractors, and, of course, our family cars, which were always dirty. The mud and grime and dust that covered our Fords and Chevrolets, our Plymouths and Pontiacs, made it plain to those who lived in town that we'd come up from the country to do our grocery shopping, get our hair cut, go to the bank, and sometimes pass on through Sumner and make the turn to the east to follow Route 250 through Bridgeport and on into Lawrenceville, the county seat, to attend to business at the courthouse or to go to the doctor or the hospital.

Sometimes people got on the hard road at the Bethlehem Corner—or the Hugh White Corner, as it was also called—and followed it until it intersected with Route 50. From there, they could travel east as far as Ocean City, Maryland, or west to West Sacramento, California, one hard road leading to another, the world expanding.

I was the only child of Roy and Beulah Martin. Neither of them knew that a little over a year after my birth, my father would lose both of his hands in a farming accident and become a troubled, angry man. My mother endured. A grade school teacher all her life, she was to some a meek woman, but to those of us who knew her best, she was a woman of quiet yet fierce courage. She also held a steadfast belief in the power of Christian love.

"Count your blessings," she'd tell me during my turbulent teen years when I had trouble sleeping. "Think of everything good in your life."

This belief in goodness is what saw her through my father's accident and all that was to come beyond it—this faith that one day everything would be better.

I wish I'd shared it. I wish that all along I'd let her love carry me. My father's accident left me perpetually worried about the next disaster that might find us. I had just enough of his temper to steel myself against him, and I had just enough of my mother's tenderness to long for a better way of living. I spent most of my childhood into my young adult years trying to determine a path for myself. I wasn't quite rough enough for farm life and my father's intensity, nor was I quite gentle enough for my mother's compassionate nature. I felt, and sometimes still feel, myself trying to walk a tight wire between those two extremes.

Maybe my story begins long before I was born, when my grandmother—my father's mother—lost two children to summer complaint, a bacterial infection of the intestinal tract, each at the age of two. My father was the one born after them, my grandmother's last child, and how could he not have felt a responsibility to keep himself safe? A duty he failed to fulfill one November day in 1956 when he was harvesting corn. The shucking box on the picker was clogging up, and instead of shutting down the power takeoff, he tried to clear the box while the snapping rollers were still spinning. Those rollers pulled in one of his hands, and when he tried to dislodge it with his free one, they caught it too. He ended up losing both of his hands to amputation, and as long as I knew him, he wore prostheses, or as he called them, his "hooks."

All through my childhood, he was unable to hold my hand, pick me up, or play games with me. At first, I didn't know enough to understand how his accident had put a barrier between the two of us, but I know it now. If anyone had a right to be wary, worried, and on the lookout for the next threat, the one he felt certain lurked just around the corner, just out of view, it was him. He knew the way our lives might change in an instant, such a sliver of time, such a smidge, in all the seconds that were meant to be ours. What a responsibility he must have felt toward me, his son. I have no doubt, despite the troubles that often arose between us, he would have done anything within his power to save me. Other boys learned to swim when their fathers tossed them into farm ponds. Other boys drove tractors and trucks as soon as their legs were long enough to reach the pedals. Not me. After that day in the cornfield, my father was through with taking chances. My mother, amid the turmoil his anger brought into our home, wanted nothing more—I'm sure of this now—than to live a peaceful life.

"Mercy," she often said when something alarmed her. Now I understand that when she said it, she meant it as a prayer.

So when I showed the first sign of a sniffle, cough, or stomachache, off we went to see our family doctor.

Doc Stoll terrified me. He was gruff. He jabbed tongue depressors into my mouth and made me gag. He gave me shots that made me wince. He prodded my throat with his thick fingers. He smoked cigars as he tipped back his head to study me through the curling smoke. He wore thick-lensed bifocals, and he was haughty, a word I didn't know then, but had I known it, that's exactly what I would have called him. I don't remember him ever saying a word to me, only to my parents to ask them questions about whatever illness had brought me into his office. He seemed to have a disdain for the infirmities of a boy like me who suffered from tonsillitis and colds and ailments of the stomach.

It was the winter of 1962, that golden era of Kennedy vigor, that time of Camelot. I was six years old. JFK had stood toe to toe with Castro at the Bay of Pigs and kept us from disaster. It was back to the business of touch football games and sailing and golfing and the President's Council on Physical Fitness, whose aim was to make the American people healthier, fitter, and stronger, there on the "New Frontier." Dallas and Lee Harvey Oswald were over a year in the future. The Gulf of Tonkin incident, which would bring the Vietnam War fully into the national consciousness, was two years ahead, as was the summer of 1964 and the race riots of New York, Philadelphia, Chicago, and Jersey City. Blissfully unaware of all that was coming, we were a country of prosperity and vigor and hope.

I was born in 1955 at the height of Eisenhower prosperity. My mother was forty-five; my father was forty-two. I would have twenty-six years with my father and thirty-two with my mother. After my father was dead, my mother told me the story of the day they learned she was pregnant. They got the news in Doc Stoll's office, and the first thing my father said to the good doctor was, "Can you get rid of it?"

I've written about this moment before, the moment when my father, concerned for my mother's health at that advanced age for childbearing, asked Doc Stoll if he could perform an abortion. I imagine that question hanging in the air of the office, my father waiting for Doc Stoll's response. I keep thinking about those few seconds when it was possible that Doc Stoll might say yes, and then I wouldn't exist—wouldn't have been the son of Roy and Beulah Martin from Rural Route 1, Sumner, Illinois, wouldn't have had the sixty-four years I've now had to know pleasure and joy and injury and suffering, wouldn't have had this life. I can't get the thought out of my head that there were those few seconds when it was possible that my parents would have been rid of me.

But Doc Stoll said, no, no indeed he couldn't do that. "This baby," I imagine him saying in his gruff voice, "will get born, and you'll just have to deal with that."

I realize now that, because of my mother's age, there was an increased chance that I might have been a Down syndrome baby. A woman my mother's age has a one in thirty chance that she'll conceive a child with Down syndrome. On the plus side, advanced maternal age increases the chance that the child will grow up in a more stable family environment. In some ways, that was true for me, but in other ways it wasn't. Indeed, my parents had financial stability, although we lived very modestly and prudently, given the fact that my parents were children of the Great Depression. They were of a mature age that led, for the most part, to mature decisions. Never did I feel as if our family would come apart, though we would encounter our share of challenges—chief among them, my father's anger.

No matter how far I've come from the country kid I was, I can never forget the family we were: my kind mother, who loved books; my wounded father, whose intense love often got swallowed up inside his rage; and me, the only child, eager to escape my life and to immerse myself in someone else's story. Whenever we drove the hard road, I often found myself imagining all the places that lay beyond it, and wondering if, given the chance,

I might someday see them, might move beyond those gravel roads, might leave behind me the dust and the fields, might finally know exactly where I belonged.

I fell in love with books and the life of the imagination at an early age, and because of that, the world opened to me. I can still see myself sitting beside my mother in Doc Stoll's waiting room, a *Highlights for Children* magazine open between us. She holds one side of it. I hold the other.

That magazine, with its features like "The Timbertoes," "The Bear Family," "Hidden Pictures," "Goofus and Gallant," and its pages of jokes, riddles, puzzles, stories, and poems is the only thing good about my visits to the doctor's office. When the nurse finally calls my name, and my mother takes my hand, I hate more than anything having to leave the magazine behind for some other little boy or girl. I'm protective of that magazine because my parents can't afford a subscription. I take particular objection when I open an issue and find that some other kid has already circled the "Hidden Pictures" or written in the answers on the "To Make You Think" page. Clearly some kids are Goofuses (*Goofus uses his pencil where he shouldn't*), and some are Gallants (*Gallant never writes in a book that isn't his*). I like to think of myself as a Gallant—a good boy—so I'm willing to subject myself to Doc Stoll's poking and prodding as I try my best not to squirm.

But for a while longer, my mother and I are in the waiting room with the magazine. Some of my fondest memories from childhood are the times we spent alone together, safely away from my father's temper. She helps me with the words I don't know. We do the puzzles, we find the hidden pictures, and we read the jokes. Sometimes she reads a story to me. Her voice is soft, and I want to listen to it forever. I like to think she believes her life has turned out exactly how she always wanted it to be. Always wanted to be a mother. Always wanted me, her son, and was glad that day when Doc Stoll said no, he couldn't get rid of it. This baby would have to be born.

"Read another one," I say to her when she finishes a story.

And she does. My kind and patient mother. I can still hear her.

"All right," she says.

Then she turns the page, and we begin.

If Ifs and Buts Were Candies and Nuts

*M*y mother was a devout woman, but she was never evangelical about her beliefs. When it came to going to church, though, she made it clear to my unbelieving father that she would indeed go, and she would indeed take me.

Sunday mornings, then, belonged to the two of us. We went to a small Church of Christ in Berryville, a smattering of houses off a gravel cross-roads, two miles west of our farm. We sat on the hard wooden pews of the one-room country church. In the winter, a coal stove burned at the rear of the church and women kept their coats draped over their shoulders. Out the windows, I could see the corn stubble poking up through the snow in the frozen fields. In the summer, wasps flew in through the unscreened windows, propped up with the sawed-off ends of broomsticks, and I listened to the wind as it moved through the leaves of the giant oaks that surrounded the clapboard-covered church.

We had no piano or organ, and when we sang our hymns, we did so in voices that seemed flat and joyless—as flat as the land stretching off to the horizon, as dutiful as the gravel roads that ran straight and intersected in a grid of neatly sectioned plots, as tightly wound as the barbed wire fencing off the fields. I loved the church, in part because I often felt lonely on our farm and there were other children to play with after the service was done, and also because I liked being away from my father and his anger. I liked feeling the heat of the coal stove in winter as I snuggled up close to my mother. I watched the snow drift down on the fields, and I let the drone of the preacher's voice lull me to sleep. Or I followed the flight of the wasps in summer and listened to the birdsong in the oaks and felt the air stirred by the cardboard fans that the women used to cool themselves, the fans that advertised the Ingram Funeral home in West Salem. I had no reason to be on guard against my father's temper then—no cause to worry over what I might do or say to make him take off his belt and whip me. In church, I was with my mother, and there she could take care of me the way she sometimes couldn't in our home, where moments of boredom or joy could turn ugly in a snap if something displeased my father.

Before I started school, I spent my days with my grandma Read, my mother's mother, in Berryville, while my mother was teaching and my father was working on our farm. In the winter, my grandmother closed the front of the house to save on heating oil. At the rear, she had her kitchen and a spare bedroom. Through the windows, I could see the long icicles that hung from the eaves. In the kitchen, the oil stove blew out hot air. I liked to stand near it and feel the warmth on my backside, but sometimes I liked to stand at the closed door, the one that led to the living room and the big bedroom, and press my hand to it and feel the cold on the other side.

"We're toasty here," my grandmother told me. "We've got everything we need."

She said I wasn't to open the door. She had no idea how tempting the treasures that lay beyond it were to me.

Each day at our noon meal, she watched her story, *As the World Turns*, on the television set she kept in the kitchen. When the story was done, she'd yawn and say, "Time for our nap." She'd take me by my hand and together we'd get into her bed, and soon she'd be snoring.

One day I slipped from the bed, and in my stocking feet, I crept into the kitchen. There, I turned the knob of the door, the one I wasn't to open, and I stepped into the cold front room, where the oil stove wasn't lit, and the lamps weren't on, and the sofa and chairs looked wrong with no one to sit on them.

I went into the bedroom, and I saw the shelves of books that had once belonged to my grandfather. Books that had outgrown their space on the shelves, books stacked on top of one another, tilting under the weight.

With trembling fingers, I pulled one out, holding my breath, hoping nothing would fall. I sat cross-legged with the book on the cold floor, and that's where my grandmother found me.

She used her flyswatter on my bottom and called me a wicked boy. I didn't know how to explain. I wasn't able to say that I loved the smell of the books, the dust and glue of their bindings. I didn't know how to make her understand what it was to trace my fingers over a page, feeling ever so slightly the lift of the ink. I stared at her, sniffling, dumb with all the words I couldn't yet read, and I didn't know that I was moving ahead to the man I'd one day be. If only the boy on that winter's day could have heard his voice—*It's all right. I'll be here, waiting for you.*—instead of his grandmother's.

"What a bad boy you are," she said. "What a bad, bad boy."

She yanked me by my arm, dragged me with her back to the kitchen, not knowing that I'd already begun to learn how to leave her—and everyone who would try to make me ashamed of books.

Two years later in 1962, my mother lost her teaching job. The school board terminated her contract because they thought she was too lax in disciplining her students. I imagine it might have been true because she was a soft-spoken woman who was sometimes too timid. Her students loved her, but who knows what mischief she might have allowed? Anyway, the point is that without my mother's income, things were a little tight when it came to money.

One evening, we took the hard road into Sumner to do our shopping. First, though, we stopped at the Bethlehem Corner so we could give a friend of my father's, an elderly woman named Elvie, a ride into town so she could do some shopping, too. Elvie was a kind woman who was always so good to me. She was tall and thin, and she kept her white hair pulled back into a bun.

We were in Ferguson's Grocery when something on the shelf of sundries caught my fancy. It was a box of things that a kid like me could use to play cowboy: a red bandanna, a pair of gloves, a sheriff's badge. I already had a holster and a cap pistol and a cowboy hat.

"I want this," I said to my mother.

She took one look at the price and said, "It costs too much."

"But I want it." I was amazed that she'd said no. Surely, she didn't mean it. "Please."

Let the record show that first I was polite. But when my mother stood her ground, I expressed my opinion a bit more forcefully, which is to say, I blubbered and bawled, and I wheedled and begged. In other words, I made a scene right there in the middle of an aisle at Ferguson's Grocery on a Saturday night when several customers were in the store.

From where I sit now, I feel sorry for my poor mother, who could be so timid, who hated to call attention to herself. There I was causing people to stop and stare, to shake their heads over this ill-behaved boy.

Elvie was right there with us, and it's the memory of my tantrum in front of her that shames me the most.

"Hush," she said, in that kind, soft voice of hers. Thinking back on it now, I can remember the pained look on her face, a look that should have told me she felt sorry for me, that it hurt her to see how much I hurt. But my injury was one born of my own selfishness. I didn't deserve her empathy. "Hush now, sugar," she said. My mother was reaching for the box. "See, she's going to get it for you. There's no reason to cry."

I imagine my mother bought the bandanna and the gloves and the badge just to shut me up. How she explained the cost to my father, I'm not sure. I only know that every time I think of that moment in Ferguson's, I feel ashamed of the fact that I only thought of myself. I didn't think of my mother and father, who didn't have the money to spend. I didn't think of Elvie and the embarrassment my tantrum must have caused her. I just knew I wanted something, and I thought it was my mother's duty to make sure I got it.

I'm ashamed to say I learned nothing from this episode. Later that year, in the spring, when my second-grade class was making ready to go on a trip to Santa Claus Land, an amusement park located a little over a hundred miles to our south, my father refused to let me go. I had no thought of the fact that he couldn't afford to pay what it would cost for me to make that trip. I just knew I wanted to go, and he said I couldn't.

We were in the machine shed toward evening, and he was checking the calibration on his corn planter in preparation for planting. I was being a pest. I was begging him—*Please, please, please, oh please*—to reconsider and let me go on the field trip.

"Keep up that whining," he said, "and I'll give you something to really whine about."

You'd think I would have learned that he meant what he said. You'd think that the numerous whippings he'd given me would have persuaded me that when he warned me to stop, it was indeed time to stop.

But Santa Claus Land was out there waiting for me. Santa Claus Land with its merry-go-round and bumper cars and Santa's Candy Castle and the Mother Goose Land Train. The prospect of all of that caused me to forge ahead.

"But I want to go," I said.

"Mister, you're breeding a scab on your ass," my father said.

This is what he always said when I was close to getting on his last nerve, but I couldn't keep my mouth shut.

"All my friends are going."

"I said no."

The machine shed was a building that was open on both ends so my father could pull machinery into it—his tractor, planter, combine, grain wagons. The dirt floor was hard packed and littered with stray pieces of wood, empty buckets, gas cans, and corn cobs. It was getting near supper time, and the sun was starting to sink below the horizon. I stuffed my hands into my jacket pockets and started kicking at those cobs. My father's decision seemed so unfair to me, having no sense, at that age, of money, where it came from, or what it took to manage it.

My father had his back to me. The more I thought about not being allowed to go on that trip, the sadder and angrier I got. I picked up a cob. Before I could stop to think, I threw it at my father. It hit him just behind his ear.

He spun around, and I could see his jaw muscles clenching the way they always did when he was about to explode.

"I didn't mean it," I said, frantic. "I was throwing at a bird's nest."

There was always a nest or two tucked into the corners of the eaves, but my father knew I was lying. I'd been throwing that cob at him.

He took a few steps toward me. That's when I turned and ran.

"You come back here." He ran after me. I heard his footsteps on the gravel. "It's going to be worse if you run," he said.

My father was a heavy man. By this time, he would have been forty-eight years old. It wasn't long before I outdistanced him. I turned up our lane and kept running. When I got to the end, I stood there, alone, looking back toward our house. I couldn't see my father, but I knew he was there, waiting, and more than that, I knew I had no other choice but to return.

When I finally walked into our house, he was waiting with his belt. My mother didn't say a word.

This scene of my disobedience and my father's physical punishment occurred time and time again during my childhood. I felt the sting of his belt on my buttocks, my legs, my arms. Our voices rose—his in anger, mine pleading for him to stop.

As the years went on, my father and I hurt each other with lashes and with words. We hurt my mother by surrounding her with our tempers, by being less than we should have been. She deserved none of it. She was a good woman with a kind heart. A delicate woman in many ways. A woman of compassion and faith. A woman who deserved to have a gentler life. The truth is we were a family who sometimes didn't know how to behave like one.

My father's response to my temper was to match it with his own. He was busy on the farm. He had no time or patience for my drama. My mother, though, knew me better than anyone. She knew that what I liked more than anything was books. What trouble could I get into when I was reading?

She enrolled me in a children's book club. I'm assuming it worked like any book club. A featured book came in the mail every month unless my mother sent back a form that declined it or ordered a different book. I'm assuming we had to buy so many books as part of the deal, and it amazed me now to think that my father agreed. My mother must have insisted. She must have taken note of my interests and talents and taken it on herself to nurture them. *Alice's Adventures in Wonderland, Penrod and Sam, The Prince and the Pauper, At the Back of the North Wind*—these are some of the books I remember from that club.

Some of my earliest memories are of my mother reading to me from my Little Golden Books—*The Little Red Hen, The Poky Little Puppy, The Little Red Caboose, The Gingerbread Man, Pinocchio, Sleeping Beauty, The Little Engine That Could*. I remember being in the crib that sat at the foot of my parents' bed. I slept in that crib until I started school, and my parents bought a hide-a-bed for the living room. I remember being in the crib with the ceiling light on, my father settling into bed and my mother standing over the crib reading to me.

But I also remember one day being in the cab of my father's pickup truck, waiting for him to come back from whatever chore he'd driven out to do. It must have been fall harvest season because in my memory, it's Indian summer and the late-afternoon light is warm and dust filled and nearly golden. The cab is a glorious place for a boy my age to be. On the floorboard, there are things like crescent wrenches and pliers and screwdrivers. I like to hold them in my hands and pretend to put them to use. Behind the seat, there's a safety kit that has flares and red flags on dowel rods. I particularly like the flags. I like to take one or two out and wave them about. On the day I'm recalling, I reach behind the seat for the flags, but I feel something that surprises me. It's a small cardboard box, nearly flat, and it's come through the mail. The address says, "Master Lee Martin; c/o Mr. and Mrs. Roy Martin; R.R. #1; Sumner, Ill." Right away, I know that the box has come from my book club and that it contains a book for me, a book my father has hidden with the intention of returning it. I open the box and find a copy of *Captains Courageous*.

Immediately, I feel as if I'm doing something I shouldn't. It's not the finding or the opening of the box that makes me feel like I've been naughty. No, it's the fact that my father hid it away in the first place, making it something shameful for me to now be holding in my hands.

I'm still holding it when he comes back to the truck, and, of course, the jig is up, and I'm in trouble for being a snoop, and when I cry because I want the book, my father says he'll give me something to cry about, and then everything is coming undone, and I know I'm close to getting another whipping.

"Just wait till we get back to the house," my father says.

But when we're there, a miraculous thing happens. My mother says, "Let him keep the book."

My father mumbles something about money and books, and then goes off to the machine shed to grouse to himself, and I don't get a whipping, and I get to keep my book.

So it's my mother, you see, who made me a reader. She did it because she loved books, loved them so much she was willing to stand up to my father to protect my right to have them.

Often, my father's temper embarrassed me. I never knew when he might take offense to something someone had said or done and explode. Sometimes it happened in public, and when it did, I found myself wishing that I could disappear.

It happened once at a store where I was putting up a fuss because he refused to buy me a pup tent that I just *had* to have. The tent, made from blue plastic, was set up on a platform high above the shelves. I must have been five or six at the time, and I was whining and begging my father to *please, please, please* let me have it.

My mother was doing her best to quiet me down. "Shh, shh, shh," she said. "Not now. We can't buy it for you now."

I was getting on my father's nerves. I could see him grinding his jaw muscles. I knew I should stop. I knew if I didn't I might be in for a whipping. But I just couldn't manage to shut my mouth.

"You want me to jerk a knot in your tail?" my father said.

The salesclerk had no idea what he was walking into. He was a kindly sort, a thin man who wore a plaid short-sleeved shirt with the collar buttoned. A man older than my parents. He had a wristwatch with a brown leather band, thin like him, around his wrist. The boards of the wooden floor creaked as he approached us. He smelled like peppermint candy.

"Sounds like your grandson wants that tent," he said with a smile.

He let his hand rest on top of my head. Shy boy that I was, I drew away from him, hugging my mother's leg. Inside, though, I felt like I wanted to go home with him. I imagined a house that was peaceful, a house with knickknacks arranged neatly in a shadowbox, a house with an oscillating fan swiveling, a piano with a metronome clicking, a mantle clock ticking, and a small dog asleep near the hearth. A house where I might fall asleep beneath a quilt in a quiet room and wake to the sound of birdsong. A house very much unlike my own.

Years and years have passed since this encounter, but I've never forgotten that man. Of course, he's long gone by now, but I wish there were some way to know his children, his grandchildren, so I could tell them how vivid my memory is of him, to tell them he was a kind man when I needed kindness, to tell them I'm sorry for what happened next.

My father snapped at him. "Who says this is our grandson? Why in the hell would you think that?"

The clerk's smile faded. He pressed his lips together. "I just thought—"

My father interrupted him. "You thought wrong." He banged his hooks together. "You've got your head so far up your ass, you can't see a goddamn thing."

"Roy," my mother said, her quiet voice urging my father to calm down.

"There's no need to—" The clerk tried once again to speak, but, again, my father wouldn't let him.

"Mister, you don't need to do anything," he said, "except get that tent down from there so I can buy it for my son."

Which is what happened. I've never forgotten the awkward minutes that it took for the clerk to climb a ladder to that platform, disassemble the pup tent—the last one they had—box it, and take it to the cash register to ring it up. My parents and I were quiet, and I felt shame settling around us.

My father was timid now, sheepish. He could barely bring himself to look the clerk in the eye, the kindly clerk who was all business now, tapping the keys of the cash register, his smile gone, not to return in our presence.

"Pay him," my father said, all the heat drained from his voice. He struggled with his hook to take his billfold from his shirt pocket. "I can't get it," he finally said.

He stood there, his head turned to the side, his eyes cast down, as my mother lifted the billfold. My father's naturally florid skin seemed even redder now. We were all tolerating our embarrassment while we waited to complete the transaction.

I felt sorry for the clerk, who had happened to get in the way of my father's anger. I was sorry that my whining had led us to this point. Above all, though, I was sorry for my father, who was always so ashamed every time his temper got the best of him.

The clerk gave my mother her change. "I hope your . . ." He paused, shoving the cash drawer shut with such force that the bell on the register rang. "I hope your *son* enjoys that tent."

I never did, not really. My mother set it up in our side yard, and I spent some time there, lying on my back and watching the way the sun turned the blue plastic a different shade, but it was always connected to that moment of shame in the store, that moment when a stranger unintentionally set off my father and showed us how far from decent living we could be.

As angry as my father could sometimes be, there were other times when he liked to tell jokes. Here's one:

>An invisible man married an invisible woman.
>They lived happily ever after,
>but their kids were nothing to look at.

I can't help myself. Even at the age of sixty-four, I get giddy from a corny joke or pun. Secretly—OK, maybe sometimes not so secretly—a little boy still lives inside me.

Here's another one:

>"Do you know where Engagement, Ohio, is?"
>"No, where?"
>"It's halfway between Dayton and Marion."

Bada bing!

I can only imagine how solemn my home must have been—how filled with tension and sadness—when my father finally came back from the hospital, flaps of skin sutured at the ends of his stumps. My handless father. My sweet father. "That accident changed him," my uncle told me when I asked him what my father was like before he lost his hands. "He was a friendly sort," my uncle said, "but after that accident . . ." He let his voice trail away, leaving me to fill in the blank with what I knew from my childhood: my father's anger.

But I knew his soft heart, too. Through our years of difficulty, there were glimpses of the man he'd been, the one I'd never fully known due to his carelessness that day in the cornfield. Maybe that's why every time I smell corn pollen in the air or feel the husk of an ear or hear the sound of dry leaves rubbing together on the stalk on a cool autumn day, I get that familiar choke in my throat—that ache that comes to me each time I think of what that accident took from him, as well as from my mother and me. My father didn't shut down that power takeoff, and because of that, we became a family steeped in anger.

> "What did the digital clock say to his mother?"
> "Look, Ma—no hands!"

The truth is, my father loved to laugh. He watched television and laughed at Red Skelton's goofy characters. He loved *The Beverly Hillbillies* and *Petticoat Junction* and *Green Acres*. People would come to visit, and my father would take great joy in laughing at a good story and then telling one of his own.

One of his favorites was about a bachelor who had a speech impediment. Not a disability-sensitive story at all, but the facts are the facts. This was the story my father liked to tell.

Let's call the old bachelor Harley. Seems he had an eye for a young lady who attended his church. One Sunday evening, after services, he asked her if he might be able to see her home.

"Mit," he said. "Kin I wok you ome?"

The young lady, unable to make out exactly what he was saying, said, "Excuse me?"

"I thaid, Mit, kin I wok you ome?"

Still mystified, the young lady said, "I beg your pardon?"

Harley, his frustration rising, gave it another try. "I *thaid*, Mit, kin I wok you ome?"

The young lady still didn't understand. "I'm sorry?" she said, with a shrug of her shoulders.

"Mit," said Harley, indignant now. "Mit, you kin kith my goddamn ath!"

The young lady heard that loud and clear, as did her brother, and *that*, my father said, was the end of Harley's courting days.

I remember my father driving my mother and me to PTA meetings at my school, a two-room schoolhouse just off the hard road near the Bethlehem Corner. That school no longer stands. Long ago, consolidation closed its doors—another country school swallowed up by nearby towns. I believe the building may have been used as a community center for a time. I used to drive past it when I was visiting. But now it's gone; a newly built home occupies the site. I've reached the age where I remember the places that used to be.

The Lukin School was where I learned to read, where I recited the Gettysburg Address, where I played Santa Claus in the Christmas pageant. I remember in first grade, when our teacher gave us our books, I was so pleased to have them that I asked for special permission to take them home so I could show my mother. I was particularly fond of the Dick and Jane reader—and I loved them even before I could read them. My mother had given me that love simply because she surrounded herself with books, because she was a teacher, because she was a woman who believed in the life of the mind.

She also believed in her students, and I can't imagine what that year was like for her when she didn't teach. She must have missed her classroom and the children who filled it—those sons and daughters of farmers and farm wives, oil field roughnecks, refinery workers, garment-factory seamstresses, nurses and aides, store clerks, waitresses, laundry attendants, and so on. My mother must have seen them, no matter the challenges that their social class may have put before them, as children with active minds, active imaginations, and hearts that could feel. Stories, she taught me, weren't just about entertainment. They were also about how to be human in a world that was sometimes sad, sometimes funny, and always complex. Stories were a way for me to navigate the rest of my life. I've never forgotten how deeply I fell in love with Sleeping Beauty, how I trembled with fear for Tom Thumb, how I laughed and laughed at the antics of Curious George, how I didn't quite know what to feel at the end of *Charlotte's Web*, and that was its own good dose of emotional complexity. I entered all these stories with my mind and heart fully engaged.

Old Yeller? Don't even get me started.

One night at a PTA meeting, our principal, Mrs. Moore, invited the children in the audience to share jokes and riddles.

> "What's yellow, weighs a thousand pounds, and sings?"
> "Two five-hundred-pound canaries."

> "What's black and white and red all over?"
> (No, not a newspaper.)
> "A zebra with a sunburn."

What could be more delightful than contemplating two five-hundred-pound canaries or a zebra with a sunburn? Both jokes rely on the element of surprise. The first forces the imagination to expand; the second pulls the rug out from under us and gives us something other than what we expected. Those two riddles, told by my schoolmates—country kids many would have considered "disadvantaged"—in a two-room school deep in the heart of the country helped us, though we didn't know this, develop our thinking skills through our engagement with pictures and words. That night, at Lukin School, the words were verbal ones, the pictures they conjured were all mind. Those five-hundred-pound canaries, that sunburnt zebra? I saw them immediately because I created them from the words I heard. The images made me laugh.

Sometimes my mother got giggly. Something struck her as funny, and her normally demure demeanor cracked to show the little girl beneath it, the one who could get silly and laugh until tears came down her face. I didn't see that happen often, but on occasion something on television would get her going, or some joke my father told or something silly I would do, and it was wonderful to behold—to see my mother, who was enduring so much, throw back her hands and laugh until she'd have to take off her glasses and wipe her eyes. How badly she must have needed those moments of hilarity. How desperate she must have been to escape the burden of caring for my father—even though I'm sure she did so without question—and the anger that filled our home.

One day, I told my mother I wanted a kite. She and my father were going to a grade school basketball game in Claremont that evening. This was the school where my mother, just the year before, had still been teaching.

"We'll show 'em," my father said. "We'll walk into that gym as big as day."

I can't imagine my mother was keen on the idea, but my father said they were going, so indeed they were. I was staying with my grandma Martin, who lived with us on the farm. I was sick with a cold, otherwise I would have gone to the game too. I loved basketball. I loved the players with their white shoes. I loved the gleaming hardwood floor. I loved the noise the ball made—that swish of the net—when it went cleanly through the hoop. And I loved the cheerleaders with their white sweaters and the red Cs on the front and the red and white streamers of their pom-poms. It was at one of these games that I first saw what, for some reason, I thought was called a kite. I'd seen some student organization selling these items for a fundraiser. The best I can remember now is that what they were selling was some sort of homemade boat: a piece of Styrofoam cut the proper shape. A mast made of

Popsicle sticks, a sail of some sort of material. Perfect for floating in the bathtub I didn't have because we didn't have running water in our farmhouse. Something I had no real use for, and something I'd misnamed as well. I only knew it pleased me, and I wanted it.

My mother said she would bring me one, and I couldn't wait until she came home so I could have it.

"Here it is," she said when she and my father came into our farmhouse. She was holding in her hand exactly what I'd asked her to bring me—a kite—but I was crestfallen and angry with myself because I hadn't known what to call the thing I really wanted.

"What's that?" I said.

"It's a kite," my mother said. "Isn't that what you wanted?"

I began to whine. "I wanted a *kite*," I said.

"This is a kite," my mother said.

"But I wanted a *kite*," I said. "A real *kite*."

My mother stood there mystified. My father, irritated because I was talking in italics and had obviously taken leave of my senses, said he could give me something to cry about—something *real* to cry about—if that's what I wanted.

I knew what I wanted. I'd just gotten confused about what to call it. I have no idea why I'd decided that the Styrofoam ship was called a kite, but I had, and now I was in the midst of an absurd situation in which I was whining about wanting a kite when I was obviously holding exactly that in my hands.

This was, perhaps, one of my first lessons in irony. Someone wanted something, or intended something, and what they got or what they created was the exact opposite. That turn—that surprise—was what could make something very funny or very sad or sometimes a little of both.

How about this one?

> A man walked into a psychiatrist's office and said,
> "My brother thinks he's a chicken."
> The psychiatrist replied, "Bring him in and I'll cure him."
> "But," the man said, "we need the eggs."

Now that's just funny. We, along with the psychiatrist, believe that the man wants his brother to be cured, but it's more complicated than we first assume. Of course (slap of forehead), the cure will come at the expense of all the free eggs the man has been enjoying. We're left to wonder about what he really wanted when he approached the psychiatrist about his brother.

How about the part of *Old Yeller* where Travis's beloved dog defends the family against a rabid wolf, only to be bitten in the process? Of course, he comes down with rabies—this is also a lesson in cause and effect—and Travis has no choice but to shoot the dog for fear that in the madness of his disease, he might turn on the family and attack them.

I warned you not to get me started about this book, and now here I've gone and done it myself. Cause and effect. Because the dog was faithful and courageous, the wolf bit him. That bite caused the rabies, which then caused the dog's death. Simple, really. One thing happens, and that causes another thing to happen. Sometimes life isn't fair. The courageous don't get rewarded. The strong don't survive. The good-at-heart don't always get goodness given back to them.

My mother, for example. This good woman, who endured so much without losing faith in my father's and my ability to love. This woman who read to me when I was young and invited me to be a lifelong lover of books. This woman who liked the music language can make. She ended up aphasic in a nursing home, unable to say words or make sentences, unable to communicate at all except for the inflection of her voice and the tears that would sometimes leak from her eyes.

Life can be cruel. Like all of us, I learned that lesson at a young age. My father tried to clear the corn from his picker's shucking box. He ended up losing his hands. Yes, he became an angry man, but somehow he managed to hold on to his sense of humor.

"If ifs and buts were candies and nuts," he used to love to say, "we'd all have a Merry Christmas."

What a magical sentence. Oh, the music it makes. Above all, what a graceful accession to the fact that life will treat us as it will. There will always be shucking boxes that clog, power takeoffs that continue to turn, dementia to take our powers of language, valiant dogs that don't deserve to die, mothers who don't deserve to suffer, old bachelors who can't make themselves understood.

"Mith, you can kith my goddamn ath," the bachelor said, and every time I heard my father tell that story, I didn't know whether to laugh or cry. The inclination for the former came from the fact that what the bachelor said was so shocking and so unexpected—that and the fact that it turned out to be the only thing the woman could understand. What if she'd known what he was asking her all along, to walk her home? What might have happened then? I feel sad to think this may have been the bachelor's last chance at companionship. How brave he'd been to approach the woman in the first place. How unfortunate he was that he couldn't make himself understood. What waits for him on the other side of what's meant to be a funny story? Loneliness? Bitterness? The ignominy of being the subject of this story that men like my father would take pleasure from telling and hearing time and time again?

The kite my mother brought me had yet to be assembled, but I could tell from the label it was a special kite promoting one of my favorite television programs, *The Honeymooners*. The kite had a big silver moon against a dark blue background, and Jackie Gleason's character, Ralph Kramden, had his face on that moon. He was literally the man in the moon, and the joke came from the fact that he was always threatening to send his wife, Alice, there whenever he was angry with her. *One of these days, Alice. Bang! Zoom! Straight to the moon!* The joke of the kite was that he'd ended up there instead, and it was easy to imagine that the nonplussed Alice had been the one to send him there.

I never could get that kite to fly. The last time I saw it, it was broken and ripped and pressed into the dirt out by our chicken house.

> Patient: Doctor, a terrible thing has happened. I've completely lost my memory.
> Doctor: How long has this been going on?
> Patient: How long has what been going on?

The Healing Line

My grandma Martin, my father's mother, was quite elderly and in poor health when she lived with us. Unable to attend church, she liked to listen to the faith healer, Oral Roberts, on our Philco television on Sundays. She was almost eighty years old and nearly blind with cataracts. I watched with her after my mother and I came home from church because I was fascinated with television. I loved the stories unfolding on the screen and the feeling of slipping out of my own life and into the lives of others.

"Just a made-up story," my father often said at the end of a program. "Not a word of it true."

I was a timid boy of five who normally tried to avoid my grandma Martin because she could sometimes be severe, and her tongue could be sharp. "Roy," she might snap at my father when he did or said something that displeased her. "Roy Martin," she might say. "Lord-a-mercy."

My normally tempestuous father immediately became sheepish. Once, after an argument with my aunts about the future care of my grandmother, I saw him leave the house in tears, and he spent a long time away, hidden somewhere on our eighty-acre farm, thinking whatever thoughts a man like him would think at such times—thoughts, I imagine now, about regret and shame and a desire to be a better man. I never heard him say he was sorry for his temper, but I could tell that he was by the way he finally slipped back into our farmhouse and hung his head and spoke in quiet tones, as if he'd realized the power of his words and was being very careful about the next thing he said.

"If you've ever been reverent in your life," Oral Roberts said on the television, "be reverent now."

My grandmother leaned forward in her rocking chair. She kept her graying hair pulled back in a tight knot. Her fingers were long, the knuckles swollen with arthritis. "Healing hands," a distant cousin would one day say to me. "All the Inyart women had healing hands."

Stella Inyart Martin—my grandmother. She believed in the old remedies, this woman who had nursed my grandfather's first wife as she died of tuberculosis. My grandmother believed in ginseng and sassafras, in Black-Draught powder and the oil of the castor bean. She believed in healing, and she believed in Oral Roberts.

"Oral Roberts can't heal," he said on the television, "but God can."

She must have seen only watery shapes as she looked at the screen and listened as Oral Roberts lay his hands to the lame, the maimed, the sick, those hands he claimed were instruments of God's healing powers.

"This is God's night to save you," he said.

My house, when I was young, was a house of sorrow. I was too young to have any memory of my father's accident, but I swear I felt it and still do, in my skin, my heart, my bones: this feeling of life separating into before and after, this feeling of being lost and trying to get back to the people we'd once been. This is the story of my family, a story I'd rewrite if I could, a story I revisit again and again, each time choosing a different lens through which to view it in hopes that I'll finally find the one that will save us.

This time, I choose to look through my grandmother's cataract-clouded eyes. I wonder what it was like for her the day the news came that my father had gotten both of his hands caught between the spinning rollers of that corn picker's shucking box, had stood in the field, those rollers mangling his hands.

It was early November 1956. If only he'd taken the time to follow the safety procedures that would have kept him out of harm's way, the story of my family would be a different story. But he didn't, and as a result, he lost his hands and wore those hooks the rest of his life. He often used them to hold his belt, a yardstick, a switch—whatever he chose to use to whip me. He whipped me because I misbehaved, because I talked back to him, because I was too slow or too hasty to do a chore. He was impatient, hard to please, harsh, crude, prone to tantrums and rants. He used words that my mother and grandmother and I shouldn't have had to hear.

"Goddamn son of a bitch," he'd say. "Goddamn bastard."

I heard him once tell a man who had angered him, "I'll slit your bag and run your pecker through it."

That was my father, volatile and explosive. I was always on guard for the next person, the next thing, that would set him off. He filled our house with rage, and now I wonder whether, little by little, my grandmother forgot the sweet boy he'd been, the one I see now in an old photograph, holding a bit of feathery fluff in his dimpled hands as he smiles at the camera.

She must have known I was in need of tenderness. I don't want to say I was a sickly child—I prefer not to think of myself that way—but the truth is my early years were filled with frequent colds, bouts of tonsillitis, and nosebleeds. My attendance record from my first-grade report card shows I missed fourteen days that year. Many of them were spent in the company of my grandmother. My mother was teaching, and my father had to see to his chores on the farm, so I often found myself sharing my grandmother's bed. I still remember the surprise of her gentle touch and how she was no longer the severe grandmother I'd come to fear. She put her palm to my forehead to check my fever. Then she gathered me into the crook of her arm, her hand petting me, rubbing my back, touching my face, rocking me gently against her. Sometimes she told me stories about my father when he was a boy. Sometimes she sang the lullaby "Rock-a-bye Baby."

"You'll feel better soon," she said. "You're young. You won't stay sick forever."

Nearly fifty-nine years in the future, I'm tempted to say she was wrong. A certain measure of misery has stayed with me all my life. People I've loved have hurt me deeply, and I've done the same to a few of them. I've disappointed loved ones, my mother and father included, and I've disappointed myself. Live long enough and you know that there's a sickness in people, something that makes us wound one another. Sometimes we do it deliberately and sometimes it happens by accident. But it happens. Again and again. It seems that we can't stop. And in the end this is why we love—this recognition that we're all imperfect, all in need of healing.

In childhood, I had no idea why Oral Roberts fascinated me so. He does even to this day as I watch YouTube videos of him laying hands to the suffering. Even though there's something menacing in the way he can grip a person's skull, the pained look on his face as he prays, his forceful and fervent calls for God to heal the afflicted, something lifts up in me, some rising of my spirit.

The people who came to Oral Roberts, if they were legitimately disabled or ill, must have seen doctors aplenty, must have been told that everything that could be done had indeed been done. They must have been out of choices, not knowing where to turn.

They must have been like Phil Hayden, who at the age of thirty-eight stood in the healing line at an Oral Roberts tent meeting in Akron, Ohio, hoping to be able to hear in his right ear for the first time since he was five. He wore a light gray suit and a dark necktie. His hair was combed back and oiled. He tipped back his head and looked up at Oral Roberts, who sat on a steel folding chair at the edge of the stage. He was in his shirtsleeves. He had a microphone stand between his knees. He was ready for business, this faith-healer, this man of God.

"Oh, God, open his right ear." Oral Roberts had his right hand on that ear. Phil Hayden lifted his arms, and Oral Roberts's left hand grasped his right one. "I earnestly entreat thee in Jesus's name. Heal the deaf ear." Here, his voice raised. "Heal it!"

"Yes, sir," said Phil Hayden.

"What do you mean, 'Yes, sir?'" Oral Roberts asked.

"I heard it open."

"You heard it open? How did you hear it open?"

"It snapped, just like that."

Oral Roberts snapped his fingers. "Snapped, just like that."

"Absolutely."

Then Oral Roberts turned Phil Hayden so he was facing the audience. "Phil, I want you to close up the ear that was already normal."

Phil Hayden covered his left ear with his left hand. Oral Roberts got up from his chair and started retreating, moving backward to put increasing distance between him and Phil Hayden.

"Say, 'I love you, Jesus,'" Oral Roberts commanded.

"I love you, Jesus."

The litany of commands continued, and as it did, Oral Roberts spoke in softer and softer tones. Phil Hayden repeated everything that he said.

"With all my heart."

"Praise God."

"Thank you, Jesus."

"Aman."

"Hallelujah."

"Praise God."

"I love you, Jesus."

"I am healed."

"In Christ's name."

Now Oral Roberts's voice was barely a whisper.

"Aman," Oral Roberts said.

And Phil answered, "Aman."

Then came the jubilation.

I remember, as a boy, being filled with dread rather than having the expectation of joy that blessed the lives of my friends who lived in happier homes. In my home, even at times when we were happy—times when my father and I listened to a baseball game on the radio, times when I reveled in my mother's kindness, times when my father told silly jokes and laughed—the normal expectation was that sooner or later, something would go wrong. I grew up living with the fear of loss. I saw it in the hooks my father put on each day. I saw it in my mother's grimace, her lips pressed tightly together, which was the sign that my father was about to lash out, and I saw it in my grandmother.

Her sight left her little by little, the cataracts clouding more and more of her vision until she could barely see to move through our farmhouse. I remember how her fingers—those long fingers that I now assume had once been beautiful, moved with grace—scrabbled over our plaster walls, our door casings, the oil cloth on our dining table, our cabinet fronts, as she moved from her bedroom to the kitchen. There she was, an old woman at the end of her life, having spent over twenty years alone after my grandfather died in 1941.

Her house was no longer her house. It was my mother's to tend. When my father's temper exploded, she and I tried to make ourselves as small as we could. I remember the white packets of phenobarbital tablets, the barbiturate his doctor prescribed to try to calm him. My aunt told me years later that when he came home from the hospital after his accident, he was "out of his head." This is my legacy, this rage. These tantrums, these whippings, these loud voices and the ugly words that filled our home.

My grandmother's treadle sewing machine, which she must have made hum and sing so merrily for so long, was now a silent thing of iron and wood that her open bedroom door nearly hid from view. Sometimes I sat on the linoleum floor to press the treadle with my small hands. A basket held rag balls the size of softballs. No longer did she have the sight she needed to unwind the strips of fabric and stitch them into throw rugs.

She wore flannel nightgowns on the days she didn't feel like getting out of bed. On better days, she put on plain cotton housedresses that buttoned up the front. She always buttoned the top button, the one at the hollow of her throat. She pinned her hair into a tight knot behind her head. She put on thick support hose and no-nonsense oxford shoes. She wore sunbonnets if she felt like going outside. The bonnets cowled her face and made her seem even more severe.

On occasion the horehound candy she kept on her dresser lured me into her bedroom, and sometimes, as quiet as I tried to be, she woke, patted the bed, and said, "Come here. Come spend some time with your old granny."

To this day, the smell of Vicks VapoRub, the taste of horehound, and the feel of a quilt can take me back to those days, can lead me to my grandmother. "Just stay here a while," she said. "Can you do that? You're such a blessing."

Sometimes I drifted off to sleep. It might have been raining outside, or a winter wind might have been rattling the storm windows, but I was warm beneath the quilts. I dozed until my grandmother's cough woke us both. She coughed and coughed, and when she finally got her breath, she said, "It's a misery getting old. You don't know me the way I used to be. Oh, there were days and days when I was happy." She settled into stories from her girlhood—stories of church ice cream socials, quilting bees, the first time she rode in a Model T. "Oh, I was going fast," she said. "I always loved the way it felt to be going somewhere. I guess I shouldn't have been in such a hurry."

At that moment, I started to sense what it meant to love someone, though of course it would take me years to be able to put words to what I felt. Love was empathy. That's what I was learning. Love was the ability to feel what it was to be someone else. I felt how sad my grandmother was, and that made me sad too.

Deep down, I loved her because I was a loving child. I wanted Oral Roberts to heal her. I believed that he could. Each Sunday, at the end of his television program, he asked those at home who were in need of healing to put their hands to their screens. He held his own palm close to the camera.

"God can heal you there in your home," he said. "Do you believe that?"

I did. I knew it to be true because once I had a splinter in my finger, and I placed my hand on the screen, and Oral Roberts commanded my affliction to leave me, and the next morning, when I woke, the splinter was gone. Of course, there must have been some logical explanation for that vanishing splinter. My mother sometimes waited until I was asleep and then gently worked a splinter up from my flesh, and I, sleeping the sound sleep of a child, never woke. But when I gave myself over to Oral Roberts and woke to find no sign of the splinter, I thought it was a miracle.

The little boy had polio, and he came down the healing line on crutches. One of the deacons took the crutches away and lifted the boy so he was sitting on Oral Roberts's lap. The boy had on a white sport shirt, square at the bottom, and dark trousers. One of his shoelaces was untied.

"Now Jesus, we ask that his little limbs be healed," Oral Roberts said, "and that they shall be restored." His voice rose with fervor and urgency. "Restore them *tonight*. In the name of *Christ*, the *Lord*."

Oral Roberts bowed his head, and he seemed close to tears. He rubbed his hand over the boy's polio-stricken leg. He felt his ankle. He squeezed the sole of his foot. "Oh, God," he said, "loosen that little foot up. Take the sickness. . . . Oh, it's coming now, son." He kept working that ankle and foot. "Praise God, praise God, praise God. Thank you, God."

The boy's face showed no emotion. He glanced out toward the audience.

Oral Roberts let the boy's leg swing off his lap. "Now then, Billy Ray," he said, "I want you to raise that leg up like that." Oral Roberts lifted his arm, and immediately Billy Ray swung his leg up. "Oh, you can do it," Oral Roberts said. He pushed Billy Ray's leg down and then tapped the other one. "Now raise this one up, son."

Billy Ray did.

"Oh, that's wonderful," said Oral Roberts. "I'm going to put you down now."

But Billy Ray didn't wait to be lifted. He squirmed off Oral Roberts's lap, planting his feet solidly on the floor.

"Oh, he wants down," Oral Roberts said. "Honey, walk on off, son. Walk on off."

I watched Billy Ray walk down the ramp that led to the left of the stage. He tucked his head in and squared his shoulders. His short arms swung at his sides. He took that brisk walk as if it were something he'd been doing all his life, and Oral Roberts, holding those crutches, shouted, "Oh, glory to God."

Billy Ray went all the way down that ramp. In the audience, a man wearing a bowtie wept. A bosomy woman behind him lifted her arms toward heaven.

I watch it all again on the video, and I think back to the boy I was, lying on my stomach on the cold linoleum floor, my chin in my hands. I still feel the thrill that came over me. A boy whose legs were useless was now walking. The practical, skeptical man I am says this isn't possible. But the boy I was lived inside the world of television and stories where all sorts of things that couldn't logically happen did. Sleeping Beauty woke when the prince kissed her, Cinderella put on the glass slipper and went to the ball in a pumpkin that turned into a golden coach drawn by horses that had once been mice, Jiminy Cricket invited me to wish upon a star, and Oral Roberts made polio-stricken boys walk. What else was possible? Why couldn't the day come when my father would lose his anger and my grandmother would once again see? Why couldn't we be like the families I saw on television sitcoms? Why couldn't we be happy?

One day, my aunt and uncle came in their sky-blue Mercury, and they took my grandmother away. She was going to the hospital, my mother told me.

She was going to have an operation. A doctor would do something to her eyes, and then. . . .

"Will she be able to see?" I asked my mother.

I don't recall her response, but I remember well the hope that something lost was about to return.

But when my grandmother came home from the hospital, her eyes were covered with patches, and my aunt had to lead her into our house.

Nevertheless, I was excited.

"Grandma, Grandma," I said.

Her voice was weary. "Yes, honey."

"Grandma, can you see?"

"Hush," my aunt said. "Grandma's tired."

I shrank away, then. I left my grandmother's room. I knew the answer to my question without having to ask it again. Maybe my grandmother would see a bit better, but not nearly well enough to call the surgery a success, let alone a miracle.

Then one night, sometime after the patches were gone from her eyes, she came through the living room carrying a cup of hot tea. My father, angered by something I've long forgotten, was whipping me on the backs of my legs with his belt.

"Hold still," he said to me as I tried to squirm away from the lashes. "Hold still, or I'll give you more."

He was wearing a white T-shirt. The canvas straps of his hooks' harness made an *x* on his back. The hooks were screwed into the ends of hard plastic holsters. He wore white cotton arm socks on his stumps. My mother pinned them to his T-shirt sleeves each morning when she helped him get dressed. His white flesh filled the gaps between the tops of the holsters and the bottoms of the T-shirt sleeves.

My grandmother, in the past, had sometimes uttered a few words of disapproval when my father was whipping me, but she'd never done more than that.

Until this night.

"Stop that," she said, but my father kept on.

I felt my world shatter, as it always did when my father whipped me. Everything swirled around me as if I were in the middle of the colored pieces of glass that flashed inside my kaleidoscope when I turned it. No center held me. There were only the lashes from my father's belt, my tears, my screams, my pleas for him to stop, please stop.

Then my grandmother was moving. She stepped up to my father. Somehow in the fog of her vision, she found the bare skin of his right arm, and she pressed the hot teacup to it, and in a measured voice, her anger barely contained, she said, "I told you to leave that boy alone."

Just like that, the lashes from my father's belt stopped. My legs were on fire. I heard the tip of his belt brush the floor as he let his arm sag.

No one in our house had ever stood up to my father, and now here was my grandmother, nearly blind, defending me with what she had at hand, a cup of boiling hot tea.

I know now my father was confused. Maybe in that moment he came to remember the person he'd been before his accident, a person of kindness, so my uncle would tell me years in the future when he talked about how that day in the cornfield changed my father. A person who was quick to laugh, a person who was generous and kind, a person who was loving and sweet. Maybe he recalled how it felt to be the boy he was, and maybe that allowed him to understand all that he was taking from me—all my faith in goodness and love. It would take me a long time to reclaim that faith. If not for my mother's own goodness, I may have never again found it. Did my father ever know how close I was to being lost forever?

Though I couldn't know it that night, perhaps my redemption started when my grandmother pressed that hot teacup into my father's arm.

He stopped swinging his belt. He stood there, a look of disbelief on his face, a look that was also a look of shame. He looked—I realize this now—like a little boy who was lost and afraid.

"Ma?" he said in a choked voice.

This was her son. I think now of all she couldn't save: my grandfather's first wife, her own eyesight, my father's hands. How she must have wanted to stop trying, to let the world's deterioration have its way, but she had healing hands. She laid them to my father that night. She reached out with her empty hand and touched him tenderly on the spot she'd burned. Her voice was still firm, and in that firmness there was love. "I said stop whipping that boy."

She went on to her bedroom. My father sank down into a chair. I crawled up onto his lap, and we sat there, the two of us. I took the curve of his hook between my hands, and I held it. He didn't resist. I held the cold steel. It was all I could think to do. My grandmother had brought me here. I heard the springs of her bed creak as she lay down. Soon we would all lie down, my mother and father and I, and we would sleep, and we would do our best to forget the ugliness of our lives, and when the morning came, we would rise, this family—I convinced myself it could be true—to a new and glorious day.

The truth is my father and I would spend years and years struggling through our anger before reaching a calmer place, but on that night, I felt blessed.

I think now of the way those who claimed that Oral Roberts had healed them came down the ramp, their arms lifted to heaven, some of them weeping, some of them smiling, all of them restored, made whole. Although their healing may have been manufactured or the result of a temporary persuasion—as this moment of peace between my father and me would prove to be—as a boy, their rapture fascinated me and unnerved me as well. What was it that I didn't trust? What was it about their dramatic healing that unsettled me while at the same time I longed to embrace it? I know now it was the fact that these people—these sick and afflicted people—were so human, so much in need, I couldn't help but believe.

The night my grandmother saved me, I held my father's hook because there was nothing else to hold onto. He had no palm to offer, no fingers to close around mine the way he'd held the fluff of feathers in that baby picture. Even now, I wonder what his hand would have felt like. I look at my own hands, and I try to imagine the skin that would have been his, the raised veins, the wrinkled knuckles, the calloused palm. I try to conjure up the warmth of flesh, the flex of tendons, the support of ligaments, the spark of nerves, the substance of muscles and bones. All my life, I've tried to rescue those damaged hands, so I might reconstruct them, carry them to him, tell him he can take off those hooks and never again have to put them on, never again have to settle into their harness and carry around the weight of them.

Throw them off, I want to say to him. And with them throw off your anger, and I'll let go of mine. This is what I've come to offer.

He flexes his fingers, trying them out. He closes his hands into fists, holds them clenched for a long time, and then opens them and leaves them open. He stares down at his palms with wonder, and then reaches them out to me.

I don't hesitate. I take them into mine, and like that, the two of us begin the life—our divine life, the one we should have had.

Bachelors

S oon I would learn there were other people on the farms distant from the hard road who were in need of healing. My father had a cousin named Dewey. He was a bachelor who had a little patch of ground, and he did some farming and made money hiring himself out to help other farmers like my father. He was a man in his middle years or maybe a little bit past them. He'd been married once, but the marriage ended in divorce a long time before I arrived. The point is, he'd lived alone for a good long while, and then one summer, he began to take notice of the woman who ran the general store in Berryville. Little by little, it became apparent that he was sweet on Grace Moore, and she was sweet on him.

Grace was divorced from a man who ended up in the state hospital in Anna, which is where people went when they were, as my mother would have said, "troubled." The mental hospital, the insane asylum, the loony bin, the booby hatch. I heard that hospital referred to with all of these insensitive terms. In my teenage years, when my rebellious nature clashed with my father's temper, he often said, "I'll send you to Anna." Even though I was pretty sure he wouldn't, there was a part of me that feared that he might. Every time he said those words, my mind flashed to an image from my childhood. My parents and I had just driven away from the Berryville Store, and I saw a man walking along the side of the road. He had on a wide-brimmed straw hat, a twill jacket hooked on a finger and tossed over his shoulder, a chambray shirt with the sleeves rolled to his elbows, a pair of khaki pants. It was a dry, hot day, and as he shuffled his feet along the dirt road, little puffs of dust rose up around his ankles.

"Who's that man?" I asked. I watched him as we passed. He didn't turn to look at us. He didn't wave. It was as if he didn't even know we were there.

"That's Hale Moore," my mother said in a quiet voice.

My father said, "I thought he'd gone the hard road. He must have got out of Anna."

In the early days of our township, the roads were all dirt, and in the snow of winter and the rain of spring, it was nearly impossible for a wagon and a team of horses to make its way over the muck and the mud into town. People like my ancestors stayed on the farm, subsisting on the food they'd raised and preserved and the meat from their own animals. They had no choice. They never set their sights on traveling any farther than those one-mile square sections marked off by the dirt roads, now impassable, that ran at right angles. Eventually, the main road got paved—an asphalt roadway—and automobiles became prevalent, and people began to move about more freely. If anyone left the area—either to visit family in some far-off place or to move away for good—folks said they'd gone the hard road. That's what Hale Moore had done when he'd gone to Anna.

I came up on my knees on the back seat and watched him through the dust, and I felt bad that our tires were churning it up. He didn't seem to notice. He just kept his head down. He didn't seem to be in much of a hurry. He didn't seem particularly happy, but he didn't seem sad either. Years later, I'd come to understand that when someone is troubled, sometimes all they can do is keep moving, keep putting one foot in front of the other, and I suppose that was what Hale Moore was doing on that hot summer day.

"Where's he going?" I asked.

"Probably to one of his kids' places," my father said. "I don't imagine Grace wants anything to do with him."

"Grace?" I said.

"They used to be married," my father said.

Divorce was an unfamiliar concept to me. It rarely happened at that time in the place where we lived. This isn't to say that everyone's marriage was a happy one. I'm sure there were people barely holding on, tolerating misery, because, well. . . . That's just what folks did in our part of the world when

I was a boy. Those like Dewey and Grace, who divorced their spouses and then found themselves alone on the downside of their lives, were the exception, and they stood out in our rural community where the nuclear family, no matter how unhappy the people in it might be, was the norm. And a second marriage? Well, as I was about to learn, that wasn't always an easy sell.

The Berryville Store was open late on Wednesday and Saturday nights. As I recall, it was a Wednesday toward dusk, a few weeks after I'd seen Hale Moore walking along the road, when Dewey pulled his car, an old brown Ford that needed a new muffler, up to the store.

I was sitting on the slope of a freshly mowed ditch across the road with a friend, practicing whistling by cupping our hands and blowing over a blade of grass held between our thumbs. It was that time of night once known as the gloaming—that twilight time when barn swallows swooped low in the sky, coming in to roost, and the chirr of insects set in, and lights came on in houses, and the air was still, and sounds carried a long way and sometimes echoed in the fading of the light.

Dewey stepped out of his Ford, and the door creaked on its hinges. He had on a checked sport shirt, buttoned at the collar. He was whistling a tune, something light and airy, and all these years later, when I recall this moment, I find myself thinking, *There goes a happy man.* He sprang up onto the front porch of the store, opened the screen door, and stepped inside, the door tapping the frame, once, twice, as it came back on its spring.

My friend and I went on trying to whistle.

Then we heard loud voices. The screen door at the store screeched on its spring, and Dewey came out on his tiptoes, a man behind him yanking him up by the collar of his shirt. The man was Kermit Moore, one of Grace's grown sons.

At first I thought he was just funning, the way men did all the time when they were loafing at the store, but by this time, the pole light in front of the store was on, and I could clearly see him trying to lift Dewey into the air as he rushed him down the steps.

"You stay the hell away from my mother," Kermit said. He was a short, stocky man wearing a white T-shirt beneath his overalls. One gallus strap had slipped from his shoulder during the ruckus. He was shouting, and I could tell he was angry in earnest. "You son of a bitch," he said.

He opened the door to Dewey's Ford and tried to stuff him inside, but Dewey wasn't willing to go.

"I've got a right," he said.

Somehow, half in and half out of the car, his arm got in the way when Kermit tried to slam the door. The door came down on Dewey's arm, and I heard him cry out in pain.

"You'll get more than that," Kermit said, "if you ever come back here."

Finally, Dewey got the Ford started, and he backed away from the store and took off down the road, gravel flying from his tires.

My friend and I sat there, stunned, and thrilled, too, by what we'd just witnessed. It seemed like a scene out of a television show. Something from *Gunsmoke*, or *The Rifleman*, or *Combat*. Two men having at each other, one of them in the midst of a violent rage, promising to hurt the other.

But these were men I'd known to be good-natured. Full of bluster and bluff, of course, as most men were. Prone to pop off from time to time with innocent ribbing. But this was something different. This was temper and threat and danger. A part of me was enthralled, but another part of me felt embarrassed and small to see Dewey, a man who was always kind to me, humiliated in this way.

Kermit went back in the store, and a short time later, my father came out and called for me, and we went home.

This was the summer that my father and I spent the weekdays alone on our farm. My mother was taking classes at Eastern Illinois University, an hour's drive north in Charleston. When she was eighteen, she'd passed an examination that gave her a teaching license, and she'd taught over twenty-five years before her school board said she'd have to finish her bachelor's degree. That's what she was doing that summer at Eastern. My father and I drove up to get her on Friday afternoons, and we took her back on Sunday evenings. The other days, my father always told people, we were "batching it." We were bachelors. We were men living without women, something I'd never done, so there were times I wasn't sure how to behave. Like that night when we left the store. What was I allowed to ask about what had happened?

My father broached the subject first. "I suppose you saw," he said.

The windows on our truck were down, and the smell of freshly cut hay, curing in the field, came in with the warm air. My father worked the gearshift lever on the column of the steering wheel with his right hook. His left one was slipped over a special spinner knob on that side of the steering wheel, a requirement for him to be able to keep his driver's license.

How was I to answer? Was it all right to say I had, to ask my father why Kermit had been so angry, to say I'd felt a thrill while at the same time I'd been embarrassed by the sudden flare of violence? I wasn't a rough and tumble boy. The ways of men were mysterious to me. I was ill-suited to be a farm kid. Most of my friends went barefoot and shirtless all summer. Each time I tried to go without shoes, I ended up stepping on something: a gear from a clock that somehow got into our yard, a tree root, a piece of glass. My mother cleaned my wounds. Doc Stoll gave me a tetanus shot and mumbled something about maybe shoes being a good idea for me in the future.

"Kermit was mad," I said.

My father stopped at the crossroads. Before he made the left-hand turn onto the county line road that would take us to our farm, he looked at me. He was one of those rough and tumble men, but he said to me in a soft voice—I imagine now he said to me what my mother would have said, feeling his parental responsibility in her absence—"Don't you be that way. You keep a level head on your shoulders. That kind of fool behavior only leads to trouble."

The next morning, Dewey's Ford came down our lane. He had a double-barrel shotgun with him.

"I'm not going anywhere without this," he said. "Not now."

He and my father sat on webbed lawn chairs beneath the shade of the big maple tree out front, and I sat on the grass near them. They talked as if I weren't there. They talked the private talk of men.

Dewey had the shotgun across his lap. He rolled his left sleeve up and showed my father the ugly bruise from where Kermit had slammed the car door on his arm.

"You can't do that to a man and get away with it," Dewey said. "Someone has to answer for it."

My father said, "You want to be careful. You don't want to end up in jail."

Dewey tugged down his sleeve. "He threatened me. He treated me like I was no one. I went home, and I sat up all night with this." He slapped the stock of the shotgun. "Just in case."

My father cautioned him again. "You don't want someone to end up dead."

"No, I don't. But I love Grace, and I won't let him or anyone else keep me away from her." It was at this point when his voice cracked, and I could see he was close to tears. "I sat there all night," he said.

I felt myself crossing into a world I wasn't yet supposed to know—a world, I know now, of the heart and its yearning and everything that tries to stand in our way.

"All night," Dewey said again, and his eyes were fierce. "Goddamn it."

He was a man afraid. A man in a pickle. He'd lived alone so long, and now here was this woman and the light she brought him. He was a man willing to risk his life for the sake of her companionship and love.

These were the people I came from. Men and women who worked hard, laughed easily, called lunch "dinner" and dinner "supper." Folks who had barely been out of the county unless it was to get on a ship and travel across an ocean to fight a war. Folks some might consider rubes or bumpkins. People who made their homes on those farms and in those small towns and just like everyone everywhere came to find out who they were when they were alone in the night, when they were "troubled," when they waited for whatever was about to come, when they felt their hearts torn by everything they wanted and everything they feared, when they calculated how much they were willing to risk.

Dewey loved Grace Moore. To him, it was that simple. An angry son? A bruised arm? Threat and injury were nothing in the face of that love. If he had to carry a shotgun, if he had to stay on watch all night, that's exactly what he'd do.

"I've been alone so long," he said. "She makes me happy."

"Then you know what you want," my father said.

"I do," said Dewey.

And my father let him sit there in the shade, the breeze sending maple seedlings winging down, and no one said a word for a good long while.

"I'll get through this," Dewey finally said.

Then he took his shotgun and got into his car, and he drove away.

And he did—get through it I mean. He married Grace. They had years together. Whether Kermit ever accepted the marriage, I can't say. I only know that where there had once been a bachelor there was now a husband

and a wife. A new life began the way it had for my parents when they decided to marry, the way it had four years later when I unexpectedly came along, and the way it did the next year after that when my father lost his hands.

Sometimes when I was a boy on the farm, I'd find the skin a snake had shed. It had put on a new skin and slithered right out of its old one. It always amazed me, this sloughing off, this presto chango, this natural moving from one state of being to another.

I didn't yet know the man I'd one day be, and I had a hard time imagining my life, especially when I was in the company of men. I preferred my mother and her tender heart, and the way she let me know, without saying a word, that it was all right to be sensitive to the world around me.

She came home the weekend after Kermit accosted Dewey at the Berryville Store, and I don't remember my father saying a word to her about it. Perhaps they talked about it when I was out of earshot. Maybe she told my father she didn't want me to hear such gossip.

"But it's not gossip," I imagine my father saying. "It's the goddamn truth."

"Still," my mother might have said. "It's no behavior for a boy to know let alone hear you going on about . . . and with that kind of language."

She was taking a zoology class that summer, and I liked to walk with her along the fencerows as she let me swoop her butterfly net through weeds—over foxtail, milkweed, and honeysuckle vine—to see what sorts of insects we might catch. If we caught something she could use as a specimen, she dropped it into a glass jar—the killing jar, she called it—along with cotton balls soaked in fingernail polish remover. She screwed on the lid and waited for the insect to die.

My tenderhearted mother. The same tenderhearted mother who killed chickens by wringing their necks, the chickens she cut into pieces and cooked for our Sunday dinners. How could this be the same woman who sat beside me when I was afraid of the dark, the same woman who sang so softly in church, the same woman who said a prayer with me before I went to bed?

I didn't like to watch the insects die, but I was afraid to express my displeasure, for fear my mother wouldn't let me go with her to search for them anymore. So I kept quiet.

I remembered Hale Moore and the way he walked along that dusty country road with his head down and how every time I thought of him—that solitary, somber figure—I got an ache in my throat the way I always did when I was about to cry. His son, Kermit, took issue with Dewey's affections for his mother and lost his temper that night at the Berryville Store. Did he go home and feel ashamed of what he'd done, or did he persist in trying to keep his mother and Dewey apart? But Dewey stood firm. In the end, he and Grace found a way to make good on their love.

Now I try to imagine what my father's accident did to my mother. Surely it hardened her, tempered her like the steel of the hooks she lifted onto my father each morning and relieved him of each night. Their weight became hers too. I see that now. She carried them with her all the years of her life after the accident, not in the same way that he carried them, but still I imagine that once he was dead, and she woke to face the new day, she must have missed the heft of them, must have missed the sound of the harness creaking as my father slipped his stumps into the holsters and she helped him settle the canvas straps across his back, must have missed the sound of his footsteps over their bedroom floor, must have missed the weight they shared.

The summer Kermit Moore tried to hurt Dewey, tried to scare him away from his mother, I had no idea how it tied into my own life and the life my mother and father had. Still, I took it all in, and it was there when finally I made the connection.

That snakeskin. The animal who had to make room for a new one. The way I cared for my father that summer—shaved him, dressed him, cleaned him after he used the toilet. His bursts of temper. The way we sometimes slept next to each other. The night a thunderstorm came, and we lost our electricity, and I was afraid someone might be lurking outside. My father said, "Hush, honey. Nothing to be afraid of. I'm here. Everything will be all right. Close your eyes and go to sleep, and before you know it, it'll be light again."

We were bachelors that summer. We had each other, just the way Dewey and Grace did, just the way my parents did. I was just beginning to learn what they already knew: all the ways to reinvent ourselves when trouble comes, when we find out we'll do anything to keep ourselves from being alone.

Gone the Hard Road

I was eight years old the summer that Kermit Moore told Dewey to stay away from his mother. I was at an age when I was starting to become more capable of stepping inside someone else's skin, of understanding that the world wasn't just me and my wants—wasn't just the self-centered world of an only child. I felt Roy's anger. I felt Dewey's fear and humiliation. I felt my father's concern that Dewey would do something foolish and end up in trouble with the law. Above all, I felt my own confusion over the ways that men chose to move through this world that was growing larger the older I became.

"People in hell wanting ice water too," my father said when I was younger and whined over something I thought I should have.

I learned that in our family, my father was the one who, for the most part, decided what someone should want.

The year my mother didn't teach, she used a teachers' placement service in Champaign to look for another position. What I was too young to realize at the time was that this meant she was looking for teaching jobs in locations other than our home area.

I'll never forget the Sunday afternoon when she was trying to help me learn to ride my bicycle in our lane. The bicycle had been a birthday gift from a number of aunts and uncles on my mother's side of the family, and I was ashamed of how long it was taking me to learn how to ride it. It was a red AMF Roadmaster bike, made at the plant where one of my uncles worked. It had black handlebar grips with red and white streamers hanging from the ends. It even had a headlight, but at the rate I was learning to ride, it would be a very long time before I'd be out at night and need it, if ever.

My parents had put training wheels on the bike to try to hasten my learning. My mother's hand provided a steadying touch as she hurried along beside me. We weren't far from the house, just down the first little hill where the lane flattened out.

I heard the spring on the screen door of our farmhouse squeal. Then my father's voice shouting, "Beulah! Phone! It's long-distance!"

And then my mother was running up the hill toward the house, and I was alone in the lane.

This all happened during a time when a long-distance phone call was a very, very big deal. Usually, people didn't place them unless there was bad news or good news that just couldn't wait for the time it would take a letter to arrive. Imagine that: a time before texts, Skype, FaceTime, email; a time when communication wasn't instantaneous, when we were all more separate than we are now.

It was a long-distance phone call that came that Sunday afternoon, and my mother was in a hurry to find out who wanted to talk to her.

By the time I made my way to the house, pushing my bike up the hill, the call was over. As I listened to my mother and father talk, I began to understand that the call had been about a teaching job in a place called Oak Forest near Chicago. My father would have to drive my mother there for an interview.

"And you'll go along too," my mother said to me. "Won't that be exciting?"

But she didn't seem very excited. She just seemed tired. If I'd known the word *resigned*, then that's the word I would have used to describe her. She seemed resigned to going to Oak Forest.

Years later, after my father's death, I asked my mother why we moved away from the farm.

"It was your father's idea," she said. "I guess he thought we needed the money."

"You didn't want to go?" I asked her.

After a long silence and a brief bowing of her head, she looked at me.

By this time, she was seventy-two years old. She was a tired woman, burdened with grief. "What am I to do without him?" she said at my father's wake. "I've taken care of someone all my life."

My mother looked at me with damp eyes, her back humped up from her steady march through the chaos my father and I had brought her as we bumped heads through most of my teenage years. That march—she only knew to keep moving forward with faith and endurance—had steadily pulled her toward the ground.

"I think we would have been all right," she said, in what was nearly a whisper. Even though my father was dead, she feared he might hear her.

So we went to Oak Forest. While my mother interviewed at Kimberly Heights Elementary, my father and I stayed in our Chevy Bel Air. It was a warm day with bright sunshine, and I, who'd been so excited as we'd driven five hours through the night to get there that I hadn't been able to sleep, curled up in the back seat and drifted off.

I woke, sweaty and cranky, when my mother finally came out of the school and got into the front seat with my father.

"Well?" he said.

"They've offered me third grade." My mother's voice had no trace of excitement or happiness. She was merely stating a fact. "I start after Labor Day."

It made no difference that I cried and pitched a fit about not wanting to move to Oak Forest. The deal was done. We were going the hard road.

Each Saturday that first year in Oak Forest, my parents and I drove to a Laundromat in neighboring Tinley Park to wash and dry our clothes. Across the street was the public library. When my mother finished putting the clothes in the washing machines, she took me to the library, where I checked out books. What my father did, I have no idea. I only know he never went with us.

Those minutes on Saturdays belonged to my mother and me. And they were glorious. I not only loved the books, I loved everything about being in that library. It was so much different than it is today when patrons speak freely and loudly, where cell phones ring and people answer them, where people who have absolutely zero interest in books or reading come in to use the computers for whatever reason they might have—some of them legitimate and many of them not.

I loved the way the librarian whispered when she had to speak to a patron. I loved the way my mother put her finger to her lips when she taught me to be quiet. I loved the silence of that place. After so much time spent with my father's anger, being inside all this quiet, all this reverence, was heavenly. I chose my books with care. For some reason, I was fond of biographies written for children. I read about George Washington, Robert Fulton, Babe Ruth. I read novels too. I read the Bobbsey Twins mystery series. I read Tom Sawyer. I read John Tunis's *The Kid from Tomkinsville*. I watched the librarian stamp the due date on the slip of paper glued inside the back covers. I took the books from her and stepped outside into the street noise of traffic. I walked back into the Laundromat with my mother—back to the chug-chug of the washers and the hum of the dryers and the sound of my father banging his hooks together, as he often did when he needed to turn one of them to get the proper angle for gripping something. In the Laundromat it was generally a Pepsi bottle. My father drank Pepsis and talked to anyone who happened to be nearby—he had a loud voice and was quick to strike up conversations with strangers—and I tried to disappear into some book or the other.

When my father read, he read the newspaper or seed catalogs or farm equipment manuals, or, later in his life, the Bible. I never saw him read for pleasure. He always read with a practical purpose. There was something he needed to know, and he read to find it.

I read to enter other people's lives. I couldn't have said this then, but I know it now. I read to escape my own life by being a part of someone else's. I read to know what it was to be Babe Ruth or the Bobbsey Twins or that kid from Tompkinsville. I read to be caught up and carried away in a story. In the process, although of course I didn't know this then, I started to empathize with other people—even my father—because I started to feel what it was for them to move through the world.

In Oak Forest, we lived in the top story of a duplex on 156th Street directly behind Cicero Avenue and its strip of restaurants and shops and other businesses. Our dining room window looked out onto the back of a pharmacy, a diner, and the doctors' offices where I would continue reading *Highlights for Children.* If I craned my neck just right, I could see the fire station. We must have gotten used to the sound of the sirens because, even though I've tried, I can't remember ever hearing them.

The doctor's name was Dr. Kluck, which was a great amusement for my father. "What is he?" he used to say. "A doctor or a veterinarian?" Or "I bet he's a real quack!"

I liked it when my father got silly. I liked it when he laughed. I could have fun with him, but I never knew what might cause him to explode with anger.

One evening, he insisted that my mother open a bottle of champagne so he could have some with his supper. We were gathered around the kitchen table. My mother had baked Mrs. Paul's fish fillets for our meal and put out dishes of browned potatoes and peas. I sat at the table, in the glow of the overhead light, and watched as my mother, who was standing to my left, tried to work the cork from the champagne bottle. Her lips were set in a tight line, and I realize now, her severe look was probably because she didn't approve of my father drinking champagne—or drinking anything alcoholic for that matter. Her father, a grandfather I never knew because he died when I was five months old, had lost the mortgage on his farm because of a drinking problem, and this had caused my mother, who never drank, great shame. She was a Christian woman who never preached, never pontificated, never looked down on someone because they didn't share her beliefs. She knew what made sense to her. She was modest, retiring, and totally at peace with the faith she had in God.

For whatever reason, my father had started drinking in Oak Forest. At least it seemed that he'd started there, because I'd never seen him drink when we lived on the farm. In the city, though, perhaps with too much time to kill and a chance to remake himself, he sometimes brought home a six-pack of Hamm's Beer from the Pick 'n Save, and he'd developed a taste for champagne. I never saw him drunk, but he liked a taste from time to time, as he did on that particular evening.

But my mother couldn't control the cork. It shot from the bottle with a loud pop and struck the globe of the overhead light. Pieces of glass rained down on our food. The fish was ruined. The potatoes and peas were ruined. Nothing was safe to eat.

"I'll have to throw it all out," my mother said, and I could tell she was close to tears.

My father, it strikes me now, was embarrassed. His taste for champagne had caused all this. A meal ruined. A light globe we'd have to pay the landlord to replace. The image he must have had of a man of some degree of urban sophistication shattered along with that glass, and I was afraid he would erupt in anger.

But he didn't. "Beulah," he said in a tender voice. "Beulah, don't cry."

It was the voice I would hear from him toward the end of his life when my mother would start having small strokes and he would worry over her. On this night, she was fifty-three years old. She'd taught school all day and come home to prepare this meal before turning her attention to grading her students' papers. She would be up long after my father and I had gone to bed, and she would be the first one up in the morning to cook breakfast and get us both off to school, and like that, she would face another day. She hadn't the time or the energy to deal with cleaning up this mess.

"You," she said to my father, and her voice was shaking.

That was all she said, but it contained everything else she might have said—that she was weary; that raising a son and taking care of a husband had started to wear on her; that leaving her home downstate and coming to this city where she surely felt ill at ease made her sad; that my father was wrong to ask her to open that bottle, a chore she despised. But she bit her tongue and didn't say another word. *You*, she said, and then she went about the task of cleaning up the mess and cooking us something else for supper while my father and I sat there, not saying a word.

I don't remember what we ate that night. I only remember the silence and the way my mother banged her spatula against the lip of the pan while she was cooking. That and the way my father kept quiet. He was ashamed. Although I hadn't done anything wrong, I felt that I had because I took on the shame my father was feeling. He was a man who no longer knew who he was. He was no longer a farmer. He spent his days watching game shows on television, eating lunch at Don's Café on Cicero, maybe driving down to Reiser's garage to shoot the breeze with the men he'd started to know there before it was time to pick up my mother and me from school. Maybe that champagne had given him a bit of a kick—lightened his mood a bit because, even though he'd been the one to bring us here, I could tell he was homesick for the farm and the man he'd been when we'd lived there. Come the spring planting season, he'd make the drive downstate and leave my mother and me to fend for ourselves just so he could sink a plow into that clay soil and smell the dirt as he turned it over.

That night in our duplex, he was far, far away from his home. We were all a long way from the life we'd known. We were in a space between the people we'd been and the ones we'd one day become. Maybe that was especially true for me, the boy who hadn't yet been fully formed. Maybe I, of all of us, was the one who could be most easily influenced by this change in geography.

We were a damaged man, his timid and good-hearted wife, and their sensitive son who had no idea what his life would turn out to be.

But my mother knew to enroll me in that children's book club, to take me to the public library, and because she did, I was able to imagine lives for myself that would one day, much to her sadness and mine, take me away from her.

—⚭—

Spook

I can't say that my father always set a good example for me when it came to controlling my temper, but in other ways he was just as upright as those 1950s and 1960s sit-com fathers who patiently taught their children the proper way to behave. Despite my father's own bad behavior in our home, he and my mother both demanded that I be an upright boy. They taught me to say thank you when someone gave me a gift. They taught me the Golden Rule of treating others the way you would want to be treated. They were always reminding me to obey my elders and to respect them.

My teachers contributed to my moral education with a seemingly never-ending supply of adages:

Be kind to others.
Haste makes waste.
The early bird gets the worm.
Curiosity killed the cat.
Practice makes perfect.
Many hands make light work.
A bird in the hand is worth two in the bush.
Don't count your chickens before they're hatched.

Given the messages I was receiving from my parents, my teachers, and my Sunday school lessons, why was it so hard for me to live up to the precepts they were teaching me?

Why, for example, did I balk the day my mother asked me to sing a hymn for a bedfast elderly woman? We'd finished the school year in Oak Forest and sublet our duplex to return to the farm for the summer months. From time to time that summer, my mother and I rode along with one of her girl-hood friends when she drove the country roads, stopping to check in on people who were sick or elderly or alone.

That's how I found myself with my mother in the bedroom of a modest frame house on a cloudy day. A yellowed window blind was up just a few inches to let in some weak light. The woman lay under a pile of quilts. Her gray hair was in a braid. Her breathing was labored. I've long forgotten who she was, but I've never forgotten her and the few minutes when our lives intersected and I disappointed her. Most of all, though, I disappointed myself.

She said, "Oh, is that Lee?"

My mother nudged me to step forward, but I was holding to her skirt, shy in the presence of this stranger.

"He has quite a pretty singing voice," my mother said.

The elderly woman patted the quilt, her way of saying I should come to her. "Is that right, honey?" she said. "Do you like to sing?" Each word was an effort for her, each breath.

"Won't you sing something?" my mother said to me.

I kept holding to her skirt.

"Can you sing 'Blessed Assurance'?" the woman asked me. "I'd love to hear you sing that."

There it was, such a simple request. I knew a lot of hymns. I heard them in church, and I memorized the ones I liked. "Blessed Assurance" was one of them. I could have easily sung the first verse, but I didn't. I shook my head no. I never said a word. My mother tried to pry my fingers from her skirt, but I held on tight. She tried until it must have embarrassed her.

Then she said, "He's shy." She slipped her arm across my back and pulled me in closer to her. "He's always been shy."

But that's not entirely true. Yes, I could be very quiet and timid when I was in the company of strangers, but when I was with people I knew—people with whom I felt at ease—I could be a little ham. I liked to imitate voices that I heard on television: Jackie Gleason as Ralph Cramden, Elmer Fudd,

Ed Sullivan, Red Skelton as Clem Kadiddlehopper. I could also imitate the wrestlers I saw on *Championship Wrestling* each Saturday night. And, of course, I loved to tell jokes. I knew how to perform. From a minor offstage role of "Tree Shaker" in the first grade Thanksgiving program skit to the lead of Santa in the second-grade Christmas show, I'd been well known at the Lukin School—the two-room country school I had to leave when we moved to Oak Forest—as the one most often chosen to read the captions on filmstrips, the one given the Gettysburg Address to memorize and recite for the PTA meeting near Lincoln's birthday, the one chosen to sing "My Country 'Tis of Thee" on those occasions that called for some downright sentimental patriotism. The fact was clear: I had language skills, a singing voice, and a flare for the theatrical. To sing a verse of "Blessed Assurance" would have been a snap.

So why didn't I?

Maybe it had something to do with the dim light in that bedroom, the cloudy day, the fact of this woman who was sick in her bed. Maybe I had no words for what surely was happening—this woman was dying. Maybe I knew it somewhere inside me, somewhere beyond the efficacy of language—down there in the viscera—and maybe that's why I balked. Maybe I was silenced by the awareness that one day not only this woman would die but so would my mother and my father, and beyond that, someday so would I.

Or maybe I was just a self-centered brat, too afraid to call attention to himself at what was clearly a somber time.

I remember the ticking of a clock on the woman's bed stand, the rattle and wheeze of each breath she drew, the creak of the springs as she tried to sit up.

"That's all right," my mother said. "We'll be going now. You just rest."

So we left the woman, and we went out into her front room where the women who were caring for her were resting, and I never sang.

"I'm ashamed of you," my mother said once we were in her friend's car.

I was ashamed of me too. I balled my hands up inside my jacket pocket. I bowed my head and felt the familiar ache in my throat that told me I'd soon be crying. My mother let me. She didn't say another word to me the whole way home. She let me feel the brunt of the poor choice I'd made.

Now, more than fifty years from that day, I still feel miserable when I think about my refusal. I'm quite sure that anyone who was there as a witness that day is now dead, but I remember it with sharp sadness and regret.

I could have sung for that woman, but I didn't. I didn't give her that small pleasure. I chose to protect myself rather than to grant her a kindness. I wish I could say that from then on I was loving and caring and full of goodwill. Sure, there were times when I was the sort of boy my parents would have me be—I carried a clothes basket into the Laundromat for an elderly woman who was trying to manage it while walking with a cane, I helped push my teacher's car out of a snowbank, and I trick-or-treated for UNICEF—but for every kind deed, there's also a story like the one about Dickie Nevers.

He sat at the desk behind mine when we were in the fourth grade at Scarlet Oak Elementary in Oak Forest. Sometimes he mumbled words I couldn't understand, and sometimes he hummed. I didn't think much about it. He was a weird kid, and those were the kinds of things that weird kids did.

On Monday mornings, our teacher, Mrs. Malley, began our day by allowing one or two of us to tell what we'd done over the weekend. The boys' hands always shot up with the most urgency—"Me! Me! Me!"—because, of course, we boys saw this storytelling as a chance to boast. "My dad took us sailing on Lake Michigan, and I had to jump in to save some kid who was drowning." Tall tales were not only permitted, they were expected. "We went to our cabin in Wisconsin. I shot a bear with my dad's rifle."

Dads appeared prominently in these stories, and they were always hale and hardy and courageous and strong. I had nothing to tell about my father. He was, as everyone knew, different from the other kids' fathers because he had no hands.

Sometimes we'd be out in public, and I'd catch someone staring at his hooks, or worse yet nudging a companion with an elbow and nodding for him or her to look because that was one thing people didn't see every day, a man with curved steel pincers for hands. Once, when he didn't know I was within earshot, I heard a boy at school refer to my father as Captain Hook, and that was a hurtful thing to me, that ridicule.

Because of his accident, he couldn't do a number of things other fathers could. He couldn't play catch with me or teach me how to throw a football. He couldn't have taken me sailing on Lake Michigan, not even if he'd been so inclined, which he wouldn't have been, even with hands, because we were downstate country people, and we didn't know anything about sailing. He had no rifle with which I could have shot a bear in the deep woods of Wisconsin. At Scarlet Oak, the school year ended in early June, and as soon as it did, we packed our car and hightailed it for the flat plains of southeastern Illinois to spend the rest of the summer on our farm. We came back to Oak Forest after Labor Day, just in time for the start of another school year, and in that way we were transients, never quite staking enough of a claim in either place to truly belong.

I had a friend named Larry, and he was a straight arrow. We were the forthright, upstanding boys mothers would one day wish their daughters would marry. Our scrubbed faces gleam under the photographer's lights in our class portrait. Look at us with our hair oiled and swept up into neat ridges in the front. Look at our chinos and cardigan sweaters and penny loafers. There we are, clean and decent and dependable.

Then there's Dickie Nevers: buzz cut so close the clippers have left scabbed-over scars on his scalp. He's wearing dungarees, a short-sleeved cotton print shirt with the tail hanging out, black high-top Keds sneakers, and a smirk instead of a smile like he knows somehow that one day we, his classmates, will look at him in that photo and feel, like I do now, a pang of regret that we never made his life easier.

It's not that we were particularly cruel. We didn't shove him down on the playground, didn't give him Dutch rubs or Indian burns. Those we saved for the boys we felt chummy with, the boys we were trying to impress. We had no need to impress Dickie Nevers. He wasn't worth the effort. He was a spook. For the most part, we didn't notice him, and of course that was the cruelest thing we could have done—to go on with our games and our posturings and our buddy-buddy, har-de-har-har while he ate his lunch alone, sat at his desk with his head down and his shoulders hunched up around his face, stood by himself on the playground or next to Mrs. Malley, who took pity on him. On the rare occasions we did take note, we were dismissive. When he told stories about what he did on the weekend, outlandish stories, we barely listened. We were disdainful of his lies in a way we weren't of one another's because he was Dickie Nevers, and we'd decided he wasn't one of us.

One day, Larry, who sat across the aisle from me, raised his hand. "Mrs. Malley?" He wrinkled his nose. "It smells like someone pooped their pants."

No one had any doubt that Larry was talking about Dickie, and of course, all eyes came to rest on him. He met the stares with a squint and a set to his jaw as if he were chewing a pencil.

"Children." Mrs. Malley stood up from her desk, where she was grading our themes while we took a math test. She clapped her hands. "That's enough. It's quite enough."

We went back to our math problems, Dickie Nevers included. Had he really crapped his pants? Surely, if he had, Mrs. Malley would have made certain he got the assistance he would have required, but she sat back down and took up her red marking pencil. For a while, there was only the sound of the clock clacking off the minutes, and the scratch of our pencils over our tablet pages.

Then Dickie Nevers farted. Not a particularly loud or messy fart, but a fart all the same. All along the rows of desks, our heads went up. Had we really heard what we thought we had? Then in a very quiet, polite voice, Dickie said, "Excuse me," and we all broke into laughter.

That's the sort of idiots we were. Not a shred of respect for a man who could own up to what he'd done, no matter how much it embarrassed him. The dignity it took didn't even register with us at the time, but now I think how easy it would have been for him to have sat there, silent, to have glanced around, sniffing at the air, the way many of us were doing, wondering exactly who, as my Uncle Marvin would have said, had "lost his grip."

Instead, Dickie squared up and came clean. As I think back on that moment now, I hope it was a sign of how he would go gently through his days for years and years to come.

What did we really know about him? Very little. What he chose to tell us was obviously a lie, and had we been wiser, more understanding, we would have known he was willing to tell us anything he believed would make us accept him.

His father, he said, worked for the government, inventing things to help spies and the like. I'm talking about the '60s, when the Cold War and our mistrust of Russia had spawned *Get Smart*, that sitcom that starred Don Adams as the bumbling secret agent Maxwell Smart doing battle with the spies from KAOS. Gadgets like telephones in shoes and guns in cigarette lighters, and—would you believe?—microphones in ice cubes had captured all our attention. We should have been fascinated with what Dickie had to tell us. His father invented such things. He worked in a laboratory in the family home, and the house was guarded by sentries so foreign agents wouldn't get a sniff of what the next great spy gadget was going to be.

We weren't fascinated at all. We were, instead, dubious.

Somehow, Larry and I figured out where Dickie lived, and one Saturday we rode our bikes over there just to have a look-see.

The house was a modest frame house in need of paint, the clapboards weathered gray in spots. The lawn had dirt patches where nothing grew but tree roots, snaking along the top of the ground, and there was no sign that anything like Dickie claimed was going on in that house at all. We went up to the front door and knocked, but no one answered.

"Sentries," Larry said with a smirk, and we went back out to the sidewalk and pushed our bikes from the curb and pedaled away.

Come Monday morning, when Mrs. Malley invited weekend stories, my hand shot up, and lo and behold, she called on me.

"Larry and I went over to Dickie's house," I said.

Mrs. Malley smiled, caught up in the thought that we'd done Dickie a good turn. "Well, wasn't that nice?" she said. "And what did you boys do for fun?"

"Nothing," Larry said.

"Yeah," I said. "Nothing. Dickie wasn't home. And you know what else? There weren't any sentries there. Not like he always says. It was just a crummy old house." Here I got very serious, as if I were filing the final word on the matter. "If you ask me, there's no spy-gadget inventing going on in that house." I stopped there, short of using the word *liar*.

That's when Dickie spoke up. His voice was low and even, and he talked slowly, as if he were explaining something to a dummy. "Our sentries were inside with me. I saw you. I saw both of you. I was watching out the window."

Which brings me to AD, age forty, on the night of August 22, 2006, a night not easily forgotten in Worthington, Ohio, a suburb of Columbus, where I now live. AD was an eccentric and tormented child who became a reclusive man, wanting little more than to be left alone.

But the teenagers of Worthington couldn't stay away from that spooky house on Sharon Springs Drive next to the Walnut Grove Cemetery; legend had it that a witch lived there, and the house was haunted. Kids dared one another to go to that house, to get close enough to touch the front door, to look in the windows.

"Going ghosting," they called it. You know, just for a thrill.

Life can get pretty blah-blah-blah out here in the suburbs. Late summer, the dog days, too hot to want to do much of anything in the daylight. And really, what was there to do? Already a summer overdone with trips to Wyandot Lake, concerts at the Lifestyle Community Pavilion, and maybe a trip downtown with your parents to the Ohio Theatre to see some corny old movie that you pretend to hate, not wanting to admit how much the grand theater pleases you with its ornate ceiling and the pump organ that comes up from beneath the stage before the movie and at intermission, with a man in a tuxedo pressing the keys. You've been to Schiller Park to drink wine coolers and hang out on the fringe of the crowd on their blankets and lawn chairs watching something by Shakespeare performed on the outdoor stage. You've been to the zoo. You've caught Watershed, that band that started right here in Worthington, at the Newport on High Street. You've had your fill of Polaris Mall or Easton Town Center. Maybe you've been to Cooper Stadium to see the Clippers play baseball. You've been to party after party and are sick to death of getting beer spilled on you and drinking too much and waking up hungover. You've eaten enough Graeter's ice cream to last you the rest of your life. Late summer—the dead time—when you're just trying to get through the days until school starts, and it's football season, and if you're Jenny Zanetti, you're a cheerleader, and you're a senior, and maybe, if you're lucky, you'll be homecoming queen, and your life will be perfect.

It's August 22, and someone says, "I dare you to go to the spooky house."

So you do because you've never backed down from anything, and besides, you're bored, and you could use a little kick to give the night some jazz. You and your friends, four other girls, play rock, paper, scissors to see who'll drive, and Teresa loses, so you all pile into her gold Saturn, and there you go.

Up High Street to Stanton and then left on Sharon Springs Drive, curling along the east edge of Walnut Grove Cemetery, to the five-room cottage, nearly hidden behind a tangle of bushes, trees, and weeds. There's a black cauldron in the front yard that used to be a planter for flowers, but now is just what it is, a black cauldron, the kind you associate with witches and bubble, bubble, toil, and trouble.

You don't give a thought to AD, who is asleep in his bedroom. You don't know anything about him or his mother, who, rumor has it, is a witch. You just know the stories about this house. You just know the dare. You don't know that, when AD was a boy, his grandmother lived in the cottage with him and his mother, and when she—the grandmother—died, it was two days before AD's mother could bring herself to let the body be taken away because she was afraid her mother would wake up and bang on the refrigerated locker at the funeral home and not be able to get out. You don't know the history of mental illness in that house: the grandmother, who was schizophrenic and had a habit of screaming out her bedroom window for hours; the mother, who couldn't accept that dead was dead; and AD, who never had friends when he was a boy, who stood on the playground by himself, the exact spot every day, looking odd with his bowl haircut and his high-water pants. A family with a history of eccentricity. A family who never fit in, who wanted their privacy, but there were always these kids coming in the night, sometimes pounding on the door, sometimes calling for the witch to come out, getting more brazen from time to time and trying to force open the door.

Let's say you're that boy, the one tormented and taunted all the way through school, the one who learns to go through his life with his head down, hoping no one will notice him, and then you're a man and your life is spent in that five-room cottage, watching television, reading books, writing out little stories you make up in your head, and that's all right with you. That's what you know. That five-room cottage, this life with your mother, who has been, and will continue to be, your only friend. What would you do if the kids kept coming in the night, kept calling out names, kept pounding on the front door, kept peering in the windows, until you couldn't help but be afraid, and angry too, because you're a man now, and a man should have the right to live his life outside the reach of bullies. Grade school, junior high, high school. That was enough. Now you don't have to take it, so you go to a gun shop and you purchase a .22-caliber Marlin rifle, following all the procedures that make it a legal transaction, and you load up an eight-round magazine, and you keep that rifle by your bed, within easy reach, in case the night ever comes that you need it.

The girls don't know any of that. They just know summer's almost done, and soon they'll be back in school, trying to keep up with homework and cheerleading and this club and that, and it'll be their senior year, and they'll want it to pass in a hurry so they'll be out, away from it, on the verge of their adult lives. One trip to the spooky house. One last thrill before summer ends.

Jenny Zanetti and the other Jenny Z—Jenny Zion—get out of the car, and Teresa joins them. The other girls, Meg and Gretta, stay in the Saturn. A white picket fence runs along the front of the property, but it's not the sort that says "Welcome to this happy home." It's sagging, and more than one of the pickets is knocked loose and leaning cockeyed against its neighbor. It's the sort of fence that says "Stay out," only there's an opening in the center of the fence where a gate would be if the property were better maintained. The branches of a tree arch over that opening, darkening it with shadows. Shrubs have grown wild and tall along the walkway, and the girls can't see through the dark tangle to the house they know is there.

The two Jennys stop just beyond the stone pillars that mark the entry into the yard, hesitant to go farther, but Teresa, always the bold one, pushes on a few feet more. It's pitch black, the phase of the new moon, that time when the dark side faces the Earth. No streetlight penetrates the bramble of trees and shrubs. No light on in the house. The girls hold out their cell phones for light, and they see the open window.

Then, in the Saturn, Gretta honks the horn. Just to spook them. Just to make them jump.

The girls squeal with frightened delight. This is what they've come for, this manufactured thrill. They turn now and run back to the car.

And then they're driving fast up the street, all giggly and oh-my-God, and they hear what they think are firecrackers popping, and that gives them another rush.

They don't know that inside the house, AD has leaned out the window with his .22 Marlin and squeezed off three shots. Just to make it clear to whoever's in that car, the red taillights shrinking as it speeds away, that they aren't to come back. Three shots to say "Leave us alone."

Teresa turns the Saturn around at the end of the street and drives past the spooky house again. This time, AD fires four shots, and then the night is still.

In the Saturn, Jenny Zanetti slumps over onto Teresa's lap, and the girls think, *Well, that's just like her, playing the jokester.* Then Gretta sees the blood in Jenny's long, blond hair and the blood coming from her shoulder, and the girls can hear her gasping for air, choking on blood, and then everyone's screaming and crying, and Gretta uses her cell phone to call 911. Despite the dispatcher urging them to stay where they are to wait for the paramedics, Teresa drives for High Street, meaning to go to the fire station at High and Worthington-Galena Road, hoping to see a police car along the way, honking her horn again and again to announce that everything has gone wrong.

Now try to tell the story—these girls, that man, a late summer night in the dark of a new moon, a lark, a thrill, a torment, a threat, and when you're done, tell me who's to blame.

Despite receiving the last rites from a priest that night at the Ohio State University Medical Center—despite being that close to death, one of the bullets having crossed both sides of her brain—Jenny Zanetti survives, but the damage is significant and the road through rehabilitation is long. She has to relearn how to use her left arm and leg. She has no short-term memory, can't even recall that night or the shots from AD's rifle. The courts convict him of felonious assault and sentence him to nineteen years in prison.

That's the final outcome of this series of events, but that doesn't mean the story is over; a story as complicated as this never is. I keep playing it over in my head, and when I do, it's rarely separate from the story of Dickie Nevers or the story of my father and his hooks or the way we split our time between Oak Forest and our farm. No matter where we went, we were suspect—too citified for the folks in that downstate farm community, too hickish for suburban life in Chicagoland. I can't claim that I was like Dickie Nevers or AD, only that no matter the friends I had or the activities I participated in, I always sensed that I teetered between rural and city, north and south, belonging and not, that I wasn't, in the language of the day, "solid" no matter where I happened to be at the time. Still, I found someone to look down on, someone whose tenuous hold on his own existence could make me feel more confident about my own.

Maybe you have a Dickie Nevers or an AD, those spooks who didn't matter until you needed them to, or now, when you read a story like this one, and suddenly you can't get them out of your head. They may be fine—I wouldn't know how to find out about Dickie; I'm fifty-four years gone from him. I hope he has a life of splendor, a life in which he gives me nary a thought. It's impossible, though, for me to forget him. He comes to me again and again, with a vengeance, and, when he does, he isn't kind, and that's what I deserve, this haunting.

See what you can do with the story of AD and Jenny Zanetti. See if you can tell it so it goes away. I'd be glad for that. I want it to be simple, so I can forget it, so I won't have to be outside that window when the bullets come, won't have to be in the line of fire, with nowhere—and nothing—to hide.

Noble

$\mathcal{E}$ ach summer during our Oak Forest years, we went back to the farm, and there I became my father's helper. Together we worked on machinery—our tractor, our disc, our combine. We cleared brush from fencerows. We harvested our wheat crop. When we weren't working, he sometimes asked me to do something for him. I slipped his eyeglasses onto his face. I held a Pepsi bottle or a drinking glass so he could spread the pincers of his hook wide enough to get a grip on it. When he was finished drinking, I took the bottle or glass from his hooks and set it in the sink. Before his accident, he'd been a tobacco chewer. After, he was never without chewing gum. Often I was the one to roll two sticks of Wrigley's into a wad and then put it in his mouth.

I remember one evening toward dusk when I went with him to check on our wheat crop. He wanted to know whether it was ripe for cutting. We stood at the edge of the field, the golden wheat browning in the dying of the light, and he told me to snap off a head and roll it between my palms until the kernels of grain came free.

The grasshoppers snapped against our pants legs when they jumped. In the distance, mourning doves cooed. Redwing blackbirds flitted over the wheat. A breeze came up after the hot day, and the bushy foxtail danced in the fencerow.

This was the quiet time, the time of almost light, that last grace before the dark.

I rolled the head of wheat between my palms and then delicately picked out a kernel. My father opened his mouth. "Put it on my tongue," he said. I took the grain between my thumb and forefinger. I felt his tongue as I put the kernel into his mouth. At the time, it may have been as close as I'd ever felt to him. I wiped saliva on my pants leg as he stood there chewing. "It's ready," he finally said, and we went back to the truck. "Tomorrow," he said, "we start cutting wheat. You and me. We're a team."

Surely, what he wanted most of all was for me to follow in his footsteps and to one day take over the farm. But there were those books like the one he'd tried to keep from me when he hid my *Captains Courageous* behind the seat of his truck, books my mother kept making sure I had access to. Because of them, I was already starting to imagine other ways of living my life. I was about to become the thing he hated most in the world, a pencil pusher, but that night at the edge of that wheat field, I was still what he wanted me to be. "He's my right-hand man," he always told other farmers we'd meet in the general store or in town at the grain elevator or the barber shop when they asked who he had with him. "That's my right-hand man," he always said, and he said it with pride.

That night, he turned on the truck's headlights and started down our lane. I could see the farmhouse at the crest of the hill, lights on in the windows. My mother was at work there the way she must have been that November day in 1956 when the call about my father's accident finally came and, like that, her life changed forever.

The man who answered my father's calls for help that day in the cornfield was a man named Noble, which I know would be a hard sell if this were a piece of fiction. Indeed, he was a noble man, a distant cousin who happened to be driving past the field when my father must have wondered how long he'd have to stand there, those snapping rollers mangling his hands. Noble's sister, now an aged woman, told me a few years ago that he never talked about that day. Sometimes I try to imagine what it was like for him to find my father like that and to know that he had to do something to help him.

He would have had to shut off the tractor to stop those snapping rollers from turning. Then he would have had to work my father's bloodied hands free, would have had to help him across the field to the gravel road where the car was waiting.

The drive from there to the hard road and then on to the hospital in Lawrenceville would have been nearly twenty miles. I try to imagine what those twenty miles were like for my father. I try my best to feel the pain he surely felt, but it's, of course, impossible. No matter how much we want to empathize with someone else's pain, it's so hard to fully feel it ourselves.

And what about Noble? I remember him as a kind man, lanky and bespectacled, a soft-spoken man who wore dress trousers and short-sleeved collared shirts. In retrospect, he hardly seems like the sort one would want to depend on in an emergency, but he was indeed the one whom the fates of time, space, and circumstance sent toward my father that day in early November 1956. *Oh, Lord*, I imagine Noble thinking. *Oh, dear Lord.*

One thing we learn as we grow older is that sometimes we have to do things we never could have imagined we'd be able to do. But there we are, and we have no choice.

No one would have thought my mother capable of the strength and forbearance that her life ended up asking of her. She was timid and shy, but she also possessed a fierce, if quiet, strength. I have no doubt that when she finally was at the hospital with my father after his accident, she spoke to him in soothing tones. She told him everything would be all right. Whatever they had to face, they'd face it together. I imagine this is true because I remember all the times she spoke these comforting things to me when I was in despair over some sort of teenage crisis. Maybe it was the bad acne I had and how I was convinced no girl would ever find me handsome enough to love. Maybe it was the ugly fights I had with my father. Maybe it was my regret over disappointing my mother when she caught me smoking or drinking or shoplifting.

"Time heals," she always told me in her gentle, loving voice. "You'll see. Time makes all the difference."

My mother. My compassionate, faithful mother. Where would our family have been without her? I wish I'd been able to repay her faith, her love, more than I did. She was the one who made all the difference. No matter how far I drifted from what she hoped for me, I knew she was always there; I knew she would never forsake me.

Then the time finally came when her health began to fail. She started having small strokes. A tingle in the corner of her lip, no feeling in her arm or leg, a list to her walk if she were upright. Sometimes she would fall, and sometimes she would lose consciousness. In a few minutes, she would be fine. But each time she had one of these strokes, she crept closer to the dementia that would finally take her memory as well as the power of language. My mother, who read to me with such a gentle voice, who taught countless children to think carefully about what they said and wrote, was finally devoid of words. Aphasic, she sat in a chair in a nursing home and uttered nonsense while I sat beside her and held her hand. It was all that I could do, and it will never be enough.

She died on a frigid January day in 1988. I wasn't there. At the time, I lived in Memphis, a six-hour drive south from the small Illinois town where she drew her last breath. Her brothers and her one surviving sister were with her. Perhaps that's as it should have been. She was always their caretaker. The eldest of six children, she was the one to help with all those babies. She was the one to help care for her grandfather when he was sick and dying. She was the one who stayed with her mother and father, who helped them with the general store they ran across the road from where they lived. She was the one to buy my uncle a coat one winter when he needed one. She was the one everyone counted on. She delayed her own life for their sakes, not marrying until my father began to pay attention to her when she was past forty. Did she ever wonder how much her service to others cost her? Did she ever regret that she didn't marry younger? Did she ever wish for more than one child? She spent so many years teaching other women's children, and there at the end of her life, the one child she did have was over three hundred miles away.

I confess it all now. When it became clear that my mother was no longer able to live independently, I never once considered bringing her to live with me. I found a nursing home. I moved her in with a few of her belongings: her Bible, her address book, family photos, and of course, her clothes. I came to visit but not as often as I should have, and when I did come, I didn't stay as long as I could have. I'll admit I wasn't the sort of man that Noble was, thrown into a crisis and doing what he had to do to save my father. It was hard to watch my mother slip away from me, to hear her speaking gibberish, to see tears leak from her eyes as she silently cried, perhaps because she knew she was going away, perhaps because she had things she wanted to say but no words with which to say them. I could have loved her more.

When I was a small boy, I was afraid of the dark. Even though I had a night-light, each time I woke in the still house, I called for my mother. Each time, she came and sat on the edge of my bed until finally I went back to sleep. Summer nights on our farm, where we had no air conditioning, she used a *Look* magazine to fan me. I'm ashamed to say this habit continued long past the time it should have stopped. Even in my early teenage years, I woke at night, and as hard as this is to say, I called for my mother.

She always came. Not once did she deny me.

On one of the last visits that I made when she still had language, I sat and talked with her. She told a fantastic story about just getting back from Florida, where she'd been at the St. Louis Cardinals' spring training camp. My father was a Cardinals fan, as had been her father and her brothers. That team must have stayed with her even when her memory was slipping. Yes, she'd been to the Cardinals' spring training camp, she said. She'd tried out to play first base, but she hadn't made the cut.

There's a part of me that still thinks this is a happy story. I delight to the thought of my mother taking ground balls at first in the Florida sun, digging out low throws from third and short, charging hard to field a sacrifice bunt, leading the pitcher with a perfect toss when he has to cover the bag.

She was so often the only playmate I had when I was young. My father couldn't play catch with me, but my mother could. She hit grounders and fly balls. She pretended to be the first baseman for my throws, the catcher for my pitches. We spent countless summer hours at play, hours away from her work, because I was her son and she knew that boys needed someone to throw the ball to them, to pitch to them, to encourage them.

I was crazy about sports, especially basketball and baseball. I remember October 1962, when the New York Yankees played the San Francisco Giants in the World Series. The series came down to a decisive game seven at Candlestick Park. I was a Yankees fan. Somehow in southeastern Illinois, where everyone's team was either the Cardinals or, to a lesser extent, the Cubs, I fell in love with the Bronx Bombers. These were the teams of Mickey Mantle, Yogi Berra, Roger Maris, Whitey Ford. They were often on the *Game of the Week* on Saturday afternoons, the only game we could see on television, unlike today when games are readily available via broadcast or streaming, and of course, they were winners. I loved the pinstripe uniforms, I loved the history of the team, and I loved watching Mickey Mantle hit those long home runs. October meant the World Series, and the World Series meant the New York Yankees, and the New York Yankees were supposed to win.

But here they were in a game seven against San Francisco, the Giants of Juan Marichel and the two Willies—Mays and McCovey—and I was stuck in school. This was long before the days when all the games were played at night. These were the days of kids in school dying to know the score, hoping that perhaps a teacher would bring in a television and let everyone watch, or at least turn a blind eye to the thin strands of a transistor radio's earpiece if a kid decided to bring one to school and sneak a listen.

All I had was my mother.

I will always cherish this memory. This is the year she doesn't teach, and when I run off the school bus and into our house, there she is in our living room, her ironing board opened in front of our Philco console, where in black and white, the game has come down to the last out. The Yankees are ahead 1–0. Matty Alou is on third base, Willie Mays is on second, and Willie McCovey is at bat. Ralph Terry is on the mound for the Yankees. I get there just in time to see McCovey lash a scalding line drive that threatens to knock Yanks' second baseman, Bobby Richardson, to his knees. But he holds on, and just like that, the game is over, and the Yankees are world champions.

This is the first World Series I can remember, and there we are, my mother and I, on a beautiful Indian summer day, and I'm so happy that I made it there in time. The living room smells of my mother's hot iron and spray starch. The windows are up, and outside, the maple leaves are starting to redden. I notice a piece of paper on the ironing board, a pencil lying on top of it.

My mother picks it up and reaches it out to me. "I kept score for you," she said. There in her neat handwriting is the box score. "Now you can see what you missed."

Each year, when the World Series starts, I think of that moment. I wish I still had that piece of paper so I could imagine my mother watching the game as she ironed, making her marks on the paper, knowing they would matter to me, doing all that because I was her son and she loved me.

I tried to do my best for her at the end, but I know I could have done better. I remember the story she told me about trying out for first base at the Cardinals' spring training camp, and I remember how I humored her, pretending that I believed it all. Like I said, a part of me wants this to be a happy story, but another part of me knows it can never be wholly that because the depth of my mother's memory loss frightened me. Who was this woman I'd always known as soft-spoken and demure to invent this story about baseball? I left the nursing home long before I had to. She followed me to the hallway.

I told her I'd come back sometime.

She said, "If you see that Lee, you tell him to come see me."

I felt an ache of shame and sadness in my throat. My tongue, when I finally spoke, felt as if it were made of wood. "Doesn't he come to visit?"

She shook her head. "No," she said, her voice nearly a whisper. "I haven't seen him in a long, long time."

"I'll tell him," I said.

"Yes," she said. "You see that you do."

Then I left her.

I walked out to my car.

I pulled out of the parking lot.

I was a coward.

I went home.

A Month of Sundays

*T*hose summers on the farm, I was a fairly curious kid. I took apart a clock once just to see what was inside it. My mother wasn't pleased when neither she nor I could figure out how to get it back together. The gears lay on the Hoosier cabinet on our wash porch for quite a while. Then I suppose I got to playing with them, and they somehow made their way outside, where one day, when I was barefoot, I stepped on the sharp point of a cog and had to go to Doc Stoll for a tetanus shot. Poetic justice? Dramatic irony? Karma? Perhaps all of the above. When I decided to take apart that clock, I meant to figure out what kept time moving; I ended up stopping it.

It seems, in retrospect, that my life was full of such ironies when I was a kid.

Take, for example, April Renevier. She was a fourth-grade classmate of mine in Oak Forest at a time when hepatitis B was going around our town. At school, we were forbidden to share food at lunch or drink after one another. April's father had contracted the illness. She was a quiet, well-behaved girl. I can still see her sitting at her desk with perfect posture, a white sweater over her shoulders and buttoned at her throat, her sleek brown hair in a pixie cut. I thought well of her, which is to say I thought she was nice and pretty, which was, I suppose the beginning of what I would one day come to think of as a crush. Like most boys, I had unusual ways of getting girls to notice me.

One Monday morning, Mrs. Malley, instead of asking what we had all done over the weekend, asked April how her father was.

71

"He's better," April said in that quiet voice of hers, and then she bowed her head, embarrassed by the fact that we were all looking at her.

"That's so good to hear," Mrs. Malley said. "Isn't it, class? Isn't that just the best news for a Monday?"

I was ready. I raised my hand, and Mrs. Malley said, "Yes, Lee?" She was smiling, eager to hear what I had to say. I was a good student, after all.

The previous week, my parents had taken me to see Dr. Kluck. I've forgotten why, but I know it had something to do with the hepatitis outbreak. I only know that I and all my classmates were all going to our doctors—all around town, waiting rooms were full of kids looking glum—and that there were needles involved. "It'll just be a little stick," my mother had told me. "Nothing to worry about at all."

I hated needles. "I don't want to go," I said, and proceeded to put up a fuss.

"Well, you don't have a choice in the matter," she said. "Don't you know that people can sometimes die from hepatitis?"

I filed that fact away. I was a kid who liked to know things, and, more than that, I was a kid who liked to show people what I knew.

So I said to Mrs. Malley, "Isn't it true that people can die from hepatitis?"

April was sitting to my left, one seat forward from my own desk. I could see her profile. I could see her face crumple. She threw her torso over her desk as she began to sob.

"Lee Martin!" Mrs. Malley said, her eyes narrowed, her cheeks drawn in with shock. "What a thing to say!"

I remember lifting my shoulders and tucking my chin toward my chest, trying to make myself as small as I could. I'd wanted to impress Mrs. Malley with what I knew; I'd wanted to impress April, too, and it had led to this.

"I'm sorry," I said, in a voice as hushed as April's had been, but I'm not sure anyone heard me. They were too busy giving me the stink eye while Mrs. Malley stood up from her desk and moved to April to comfort her. I knew how thoughtless and cruel I'd been, even though I hadn't intended to be. I wanted Mrs. Malley to know how smart I was. I wanted April to like me because I was taking an interest in her life. But now I felt like everyone was looking at me as if I were Snidely Whiplash from the Dudley Do-Right cartoon, or Boris Badenov from *The Rocky and Bullwinkle Show*, or Simon

Bar Sinister from *Underdog*. I'd intended to be the humble and lovable Shoe-shine Boy, the quiet dog who turned into the superhero. I'd intended April to be my Sweet Polly Purebred. But that's not what happened at all.

Mrs. Malley put her hand on April's back and patted it gently. "There, there," she said. "There, there."

And all the while she kept her eyes narrowed at me as if to say, *How could you?*

My mother and father always encouraged me to do well in school. I was a teacher's son, for Pete's sake. How would it have looked if I were a dummy?

And speaking of dummies, one of my favorite television shows in those days was *The Paul Winchell Show*. He was the ventriloquist who had the dummies Jerry Mahoney and Knucklehead Smiff. He was also an inventor, and he was the first person to build and patent a mechanical heart.

My own heart, though I wouldn't know this for a number of years, was defective. One Sunday morning, when I was a few weeks away from my fifty-seventh birthday, I came up from lifting weights in the basement, and while eating breakfast, I suffered a stroke. My vision closed in at the edges for a moment and then cleared. I couldn't move my right arm. My right leg was a dead weight. My tongue was thick in my mouth. Whatever words it held came out in grunts and moans. I tried to push myself up from my chair, but I couldn't. Luckily, my then wife was home, and she was quick to call 911. Soon I was on my way to the hospital. I was about to learn all sorts of things about the human body and medicine that only moments before I'd had neither the need nor the desire to know.

I've always been the sort who wants to avoid thinking about what's actually going on inside my body. To spend time contemplating the workings of liver and kidney and lungs—to dwell on the fact that my brain, my digestive tract, my nervous system, and my heart all have jobs to do—is to invite a malfunction. If I don't think about what's going on in there, everything will keep clicking along in fine shape.

A marvelous drug exists. Tissue plasminogen activator—tPA, for short. It's actually a protein that comes from endothelial cells that line the blood vessels. It acts as a catalyst in the conversion of plasminogen to plasmin, the major enzyme that breaks down blood clots. A clot-buster.

The neurologist at the emergency room told me he wanted to give me tPA. He said there was a small chance that it would cause a bleed in my brain, but all in all, it was my best chance for recovery. A clot had somehow formed and then traveled to the left side of my brain. Now we were going to try to bust that clot and make it go away. The neurologist wore a bow tie and carried a leather bag the size and shape of a lunch box. Inside, I would find out as the days went on, were his instruments: tuning fork, penlight, reflex hammer, ophthalmoscope, tongue blades. He was tidy and exuded an air of confident nerdiness. I agreed to the tPA.

I was born on a Sunday morning in October. According to the old fortune-telling rhyme, I was a child meant to be bonny and blithe and good and gay. Born on the Sabbath day, a time of rest and worship, a time meant for my mother and me.

How long had it been since my father had gone to church? Not in a month of Sundays, which I knew, even as a child, was a very, very long time.

I have to think he always believed—believed in some sort of redemption, some sort of grace, something that waited for him on the other side of his accident. I try to make sense of the story of our days—the anger, the love, the struggle, the yearning.

Sunday afternoons, those summers on the farm, my father would say, "Let's go for a drive." We'd stop at the houses of people I didn't know, many of them elderly and infirm, folks my parents knew, and I'd try to behave myself while we sat in dimly lit living rooms with cuckoo clocks on the walls or feeble dogs whimpering in their sleep or pianos that no one played because the children who had learned to play them were grown and gone. "It's a misery," a woman said once—a widow woman who lived alone in a farmhouse that smelled of the cracked linoleum floors, the old wallpaper, the worn quilt across her legs. "Just a misery," she said, and though she was talking about the cold she'd been suffering, I somehow knew she was also talking about a life lived alone.

I knew what it was to be alone. An only child, I spent countless hours entertaining myself. I made up all sorts of games. I read. I watched television. I walked back into the woods on our farm to see what I could see. Sometimes, when loneliness became too much for me, I stood in the yard and looked across the field to the next farm to the north, hoping that I might see the children who lived there moving about their yard—or better yet, setting out across that field to come and play with me. Sometimes, bored, I'd whine that I didn't have anything to do.

"You want something to do?" my father would say in his gruff voice. "Well, Mister, I can give you something to do."

Those summers, I rose early to do whatever my father needed done: grease machinery; tote buckets of soybeans to the planter boxes whenever he needed them filled in order to keep sowing a field; walk the rows of that field weeks later, hoe in hand, cutting out pokeberry and jimson weed. I remember one afternoon when clouds gathered over the field and the air smelled like rain, and my father finally said, "C'mon," and we headed for our truck.

We drove up our lane and parked the truck in the farmyard and made sure the windows were up. We stepped up onto our front porch, and he told me to fetch us Pepsi-Colas. We sat in folding lawn chairs and drank, watching the rain come across the fields and move up our lane, until finally it was upon us and we had to scoot our chairs a little farther back on the porch. The rain dripped from the leaves of the maple tree in our front yard. The wind came up and the air cooled, and we had nothing to do but to sit and watch as the rain kept falling. I remember the ecstasy of it. I remember the release from labor. I remember my father saying, "Just look at it come down." And that's what we did; we sat there and watched it rain. Sometimes in the field, he'd lift his head and look off toward the horizon. "Hear them?" he'd say, and I'd listen to the call of mourning doves. "Rain," he'd say, and then he'd be still, and in his silence, I'd feel his hope, his longing. I'd know his want. Now when I think back on these moments, it seems to me that it was a want born from that moment in the cornfield when the snapping rollers of the picker's shucking box caught first one hand, and then the other, that moment he'd always wished he could change. "Just listen to them calling for rain," he'd say in a whisper those days when the mourning doves were cooing. "Mercy, just listen."

One Sunday night when we were living on the farm for the summer, a storm blew in, the rain coming in gusts that rattled against our windows—great claps of thunder and lightning that lit up the outside when it flashed. We lost our electricity, and my mother lit a kerosene lamp, and we sat around it at our kitchen table while it rained and rained. It rained so hard, and the noise of it against our roof was so loud, we hardly said a word. Then my father spoke. He said, "God promised he'd never again destroy the earth with a flood." In that instant, my father became strange to me. I had no idea that he knew anything from the Bible at all, and hearing him refer to the scripture, I glimpsed a part of him that mystified me. It would take years for me to fully know that part of him, the part that believed. I'd see it eventually when he'd start attending church with my mother and me. I'd see it on a Sunday night in winter when he'd answer the preacher's invitation, asking to be forgiven for his sins. Now I see it in what he left behind when he died. The pages of a prayer he wrote in his shaky scrawl so he'd be prepared to deliver it in church. *Dear Heavenly Father,* that prayer begins. *We come before thee at this time thanking you for the first day of the week.* His New Testament, the corners of the pages creased from where he clamped them between the pincers of his hooks. I see how desperately he wanted to hold on to his faith. I can only imagine now that he must have let it go after his accident, and it took a long time for him to find it again.

I still wake sometimes on Sunday mornings with the feeling that there's somewhere I'm supposed to be. I call back the memory of the churches of my childhood: the hard wooden pews, the dusty smell of the hymnals, the thimble-sized communion cups half-full of Welch's grape juice, the saltine cracker from which the believers broke a piece of the body of Christ, the red-edged pages of the New Testament, the preacher extending the invitation to salvation—*Jesus is waiting. Won't you come to him now?* I was fifteen when I accepted the call, and I still remember the feeling that filled me after my baptism, this feeling of life starting again, of all my wrong steps being cleansed, of every sin forgiven. This was love, my mother told me. This was Christ's love. Although I eventually dropped away from the fold, and remain outside it even today, I never forgot that lesson. I never forgot that when you truly and wholly love someone, you forgive them for falling short, forgive them the injuries they bring you, forgive them for being less than what you want them to be. All the while I basked in the warm comfort of this new life after my baptism, I began to see how my mother's faith—her refusal to stop loving my father no matter the ugliness of the temper that sprang up in him after his accident—might just be enough to save us.

In the last years of my mother's life, when I lived away from her, we had the habit of talking on the phone on Sunday afternoons or writing letters to each other. My father was dead, and she'd moved into her widowhood. I know she would have preferred to have me closer to her, but she rarely complained about the distance. Instead, she stuck to the facts of her life after my father's death. In letters and during phone calls, she left me with an indelible impression of a life lived alone: A boy from the church was mowing her yard. She was having new countertops put on. One of her friends had taken her to Vincennes to do some shopping and to eat at the Sirloin Stockade Steakhouse. Only rarely did she make reference to the fact that I'd left the church. "With my heart full of love," she wrote in one letter, "I will say if you could only really get interested in church, things would be perfect!" My mother wasn't a woman who spoke or wrote in sentences that deserved exclamation points. Her use of one in this letter is evidence of how much she longed for my return. When she was finally aphasic in the nursing home, my aunt and uncle and cousin would visit her on Sundays. When they were ready to leave, they would stand in a circle, hands clasped, and recite the Lord's Prayer. My mother, who could no longer put words into sentences, would recite every line without a glitch. Even then, her faith endured.

From one of my mother's Sunday letters to me: "The little garden I have planted just stands there. No potatoes ever came up. I don't know if it will grow when it warms up or not. If it does, we might have some spinach or lettuce when you come home. But I can't promise any. I've been using onions from those I set out last fall. I want to get some cabbage and cauliflower as soon as the stores get their plants."

What I hear beneath her words: My life is barren, but still I hope. I see the truth of my days, but still I have faith. Always, faith.

At the hospital, as they administered the tPA, I knew I had no choice but to put myself in the hands of this doctor whose bow tie and shiny skin reminded me of Paul Winchell's dummy, Jerry Mahoney. I couldn't help wondering, though, if I was also in my mother's hands—if the stir of air I felt around me was her spirit come to tell me everything would be all right if only I'd believe, if only I'd call on God to heal me. And so I began to say a silent prayer. "Please, dear God," I said, and then I stopped, unsure of what should come next. Then I remembered what my mother used to tell me those days when I felt lost within my father's rage: "Tell God what you want. Ask him to help you, and he will."

I remember when I was a very small child, she read to me from a Big Golden Book, *Dale Evans Prayer Book for Children*. Dale Evans, "Queen of the West," the wife of Roy Rogers, the square-dealing "King of the Cowboys." They stood for all things decent and right, and as hokey as that may seem these days, I still look back with great affection at the boy I was and my mother's attempts to keep reminding me of everything that was good in the world. She was no Dale Evans, mind you. She couldn't do rope tricks, couldn't ride, couldn't sing worth a lick. But she was a mother who wanted her son to know he was loved. From this book, I learned my first prayer of gratitude: "God is great and God is good / And we thank him for our food." And I learned how to ask God to take care of me: "Now I lay me down to sleep / I pray the Lord my soul to keep." No matter how far I'd eventually travel from that simple faith, I'd never be able to completely forsake it. I'd carry it with me through everything that lay ahead. I wish my mother were still alive so I could tell her that her efforts weren't in vain; I can still hear her gentle voice reading from that prayer book as she sat on the edge of my bed, and I repeated the words she said, taking them in, feeling the goodness of her love.

My first night in the hospital, I lay awake, poleaxed by the fact of my stroke, stunned beyond belief that this had happened to me. Even though the tPA had done its job, dissolving the clot and giving me back the power of speech and the use of the right side of my body, I was in a very strange place of being "the man who had a stroke," and I didn't know how to deal with that. I knew that the next day I'd have to let my colleagues and students know what happened, and that grieved me because I've never wanted to be the person who needed help or sympathy. I didn't know how long I'd be in the hospital or whether I'd fully recover from the stroke. I didn't know what the tests to come would reveal. I was vulnerable and uncertain, afraid to go to sleep for fear that another stroke might come.

I thought of my father at the moment when he knew his hands were caught in the rollers of that picker's shucking box and no one was nearby to help him. I thought of my mother living alone in her widowhood and suffering who knows how many small strokes, the transient ischemic attacks (TIAs) that nibbled at her brain until she slipped into dementia and became lost to me forever. I thought of how we were a family—always a family even when it appeared we were coming apart—and how much faith it took in one another to keep believing that one day things would be better. "Your father loves you," my mother kept telling me in those dark teenage years when he and I were always fighting. "And you love him." It took this faith in our better parts to give us confidence in the future; that's what my mother was telling me. "You wouldn't get so angry with each other if you didn't." I thought of all of this as I lay in my hospital bed and asked a God I still wasn't convinced was there to watch over me.

A patent foramen ovale, that's what caused my stroke. A hole between the atria of my heart that allowed a blood clot to shunt from right to left, as it wasn't supposed to be able to do, and travel up an artery to my brain. We all have this foramen ovale when we're in the womb, a hole in the atrial septum, the muscular wall between the atria of the heart. A flap of tissue allows blood to flow from the right atrium to the left. Since we get our oxygen from the placenta, we don't need the blood to pass through our lungs. We have a layer of tissue that acts as a valve over the foramen ovale. After we're born, the pressure in the right side of the heart drops when the lungs start working, and this decrease in pressure causes the foramen ovale to close entirely. In approximately 25 percent of the population, though, the foramen ovale doesn't seal, and then it's known as a patent foramen ovale, or PFO. I listened to this explanation from a cardiologist. He told me he could close it. He could correct this congenital defect. He didn't know that I have an affinity for puns. He didn't know that I kept myself from saying, "Gee, Doc, are you saying we should fix my *holy* heart?"

One Sunday night, a few weeks after I was baptized, my father went forward at the invitation. He stomped up the aisle, determined. His coming forward was surprising, and yet it somehow seemed inevitable. I'd come to church that night not expecting this at all, but once my father took that first step, it seemed to me like the last steps of a journey that he'd been on for years since his accident. I recalled the night of the storm when I was a much younger boy and the way he made reference to God promising never again to end the world with a flood. I remembered a moment sometime after that night when I was riding in the truck with my father and he began singing the old hymn, "Rescue the Perishing." I thought of the recent evenings he'd spent in conversation with one of the church's elders when my mother invited him and his wife to supper. My father asked questions about heaven, about redemption, about how faith could be a certainty. Now he was coming forward. My mother kept singing in her timid, off-key voice, giving no sign that what she had long hoped for had finally arrived. She kept her eyes on her hymnal. The song was "Just as I Am," and there was my father giving himself over to the preacher who put his hand on his shoulder and leaned in to say something to him. When the singing ended and the preacher asked my father if he'd come to accept Jesus Christ as his savior, my father said, "Yes." How odd it was to watch the preacher immerse him in the baptistery and how unusual it felt in our home later that night when we were all lying down to sleep. I remember the sounds of that house—the click of the wall furnace; the popping of the roof joists, disturbed by the cold; my mother and my father's voices making a low murmur behind their bedroom door. What did they say to each other that night? Did my father say he was sorry for how angry he'd been over the years? Did he say he knew my mother deserved none of that? Did she tell him to hush, to not give it any worry, to go to sleep? I imagine the two of them, just a little older than I am now, these two people who had survived so much, turning now toward the last years of their time together with renewed hope.

The next morning, when I woke, my mother was in the kitchen, her radio playing softly. My father's eggs were in the frying pan. My CoCo Wheats were ready. Outside, the watery light was breaking in the east. "Twelve degrees," my mother said. "Better bundle up for your walk to school." Just like it was any other day. I saw no signs that our lives had been transformed.

Then my father joined me at the breakfast table, and he stopped me before I could start eating my hot cereal. "I reckon I should say a prayer," he said. Then he bowed his head. My mother closed her eyes, and finally, so did I, and I listened to my father's voice—that voice I'd heard filled with anger so many times—saying a prayer of thanksgiving, thanking God for the food my mother had prepared and asking him to be with each of us through our day, to offer us guidance and to forgive us of our sins. "Amen," he said, and I wanted to stay there forever, gathered around that table with my mother and father, the three of us, a family.

I know I'm a lucky man. When I left the hospital after my two-day stay, the nurses at their station all watched me go with smiles on their faces. "This just doesn't happen," one of them told me when she was going over my discharge orders. "Once someone comes to us, they hardly ever leave without some sort of impairment."

Another nurse told me, "I know you didn't want to have a stroke, but the doctors, the medicines, everything we know now? It's a time when we can do so much."

Luck? Modern medical science? A little of both? In my more rational moments, I listen to what the nurse told me about the advancements in the treatment of strokes that came to bear in my favor. I listen to my family doctor, who tells me everything happened just the way it should have, from the 911 call to the ambulance transport to the tPA. I tell myself I was saved by this proper sequence of medical care. I'll tell myself the same thing nearly three months later, when my cardiologist will close my PFO by inserting a double-ringed mesh occluder on each side of the atrial septum, thereby repairing the defect with which I was born. But as I watch the screen where I can see him deliver the occluder via a catheter threaded through a vein in my groin—when I watch him tug on my heart—I say a prayer just in case he needs a little extra help.

Just this morning, I woke imagining that I heard the sound of my mother's wringer washer churning, as I often did in our farmhouse on Saturday mornings those days when I'd yet to start school and had to spend the weekdays with my grandmother while my mother was teaching. The sound of that washer was a comfort to me because it told me my mother was home and would be all that day and all the next one, those blessed Saturdays and Sundays. Suddenly, I'm remembering how she called each load of laundry "a rubbing." I might hear her tell someone at church, "I did three rubbings of clothes." *Three rubbings of clothes*, I'd say to myself. Now, twenty-five years after her death, I say it again—*three rubbings*—just for the pleasure of imagining her saying it, and it's as if she's just on the other side of the door. For a moment, I feel I can open it and step through a veil of time between my bedroom and the kitchen of our farmhouse where my mother is putting my breakfast on the table and telling me to bow my head. "Say your prayer," she tells me, and because I trust her, because I believe she won't let anything bad happen to me ever, I do. "God is great, God is good." I say the words my mother gave me, her bonny child, her Sunday's child. I say the words, and for a moment I'm blessed with faith, blessed because she's left no room, no reason, for doubt.

There will always be a part of me that will wish for the certainty of the boy my mother taught to believe. Even now, seven years after my stroke, I say my prayers and want to believe that God watches over me, keeping me safe and free from harm. I can't forget, though, that neither my parents' faith nor their prayers could save them in the end. My father's heart stopped while he was mowing the grass on a hot day at the end of July. My mother, who rarely gave into emotion, wept over his casket. Six years later, she died in that nursing home, surrounded by her brothers and sisters. I received word of her death by telephone on a cold and snowy afternoon in January. As I drove north from Memphis that night, the stars came out, and I thought about my mother's spirit and wondered where it had gone. I wanted to believe it lifted into the atmosphere, became an energy that found its way to whatever attracted it—to rivers and leaves, to other people, to clouds and the very stars above me, and other planets, maybe, and if that was the case, then why couldn't it keep rising? Why couldn't it exist in a place called heaven? Even now, as I recall the uncertainty that my father's anger brought us, I remember the way my mother told me to count my blessings, to keep looking up, to trust in what was to come. *I do*, I tell myself again and again in the days following my stroke, until the voice inside me is no longer mine but that of someone I don't know, someone I want to believe. *I do, I do, I do.*

Imposters

During the six years I lived in Oak Forest, I found myself caught between two cultures, not fully fitting into either one. I was no longer the right kind of boy for southeastern Illinois. My friends there called me "city slicker" when I went back on holidays and for the summer. And I wasn't quite right for Oak Forest. I wasn't quite as citified as my friends. I remember one Sunday when we came home from church and found a boy named Bob sitting on the sidewalk outside our front door. He was a boy, a friend of mine, who was often left to roam with no thoughts of concern from his mother, and on this day he'd decided to pay me a visit.

"Have you had dinner?" my mother asked him.

It was a bright fall day, and he shielded his eyes with his hand as he stared up at her, his mouth hanging open. He had a puzzled look. "Lunch," I said, using the word for the noon meal that everyone up north used.

"I had toast for breakfast," he said.

"That's not much." My mother offered him her hand, and he took it and stood up. "You must be hungry."

He shrugged. "I'm OK."

But it was clear he was lying. I heard his stomach rumble and growl. Obviously, the toast he'd eaten for breakfast had long ago stopped satisfying him.

This was the first of many Sundays when we'd come home from church and find him waiting. He'd have *his* chair at our table. He'd eat as if he were starving. But that first Sunday he was shy.

"You'll eat with us," my father said.

And when the dishes were all on the table, Bob sat with his hands in his lap, looking down at his feet. The laces of his black Keds high-tops had knots in them from where they'd snapped and been pieced back together. He had on a red-and-white-striped cardigan with a hole in one elbow. Finally, at my mother's urging, he took a small piece of meat loaf and a dab of green beans.

"Better get you some mashed taters," my father said.

Bob giggled. "Taters," he said.

"Don't you know what taters are?" my father asked.

Bob laughed harder. "Taters," he said again, and I felt like a curtain had been pulled back to reveal the hillbillies we surely were.

Those years in Oak Forest, I did my best to be an ideal suburban boy. I became a fan of all the Chicago sports teams, even watching hockey for the first time in my life. But I didn't own skates or a hockey stick—I didn't even know how to skate—and I spent weekends in winter watching my friends play on the frozen lagoon. I'd never known what a lagoon was, nor a slough. I knew ponds and creeks. I was well aware that beneath the surface I was the kid from the country who went to a two-room school and lived in an old farmhouse that had no running water. I was the kid who went to the bathroom in a chamber pot at night, a pot that got emptied at our outhouse the next morning. I was that kid. All along, beneath the WLS Radio–listening, basketball-playing, washroom-going, lagoon-visiting, WGN TV–watching, Robert Hall– and Zayre-shopping honor student I was, I was the kid who shit in a pot, ate dinner at noon, went barefoot all summer, and took a baby pig to bed one winter night when it got loose in our house. (It'd been so cold my mother and father had brought the litter into the house to cut their teeth so they wouldn't hurt the sow when they sucked.) I was that boy—the boy who shit in a pot and slept with pigs.

But I kept trying my best to hide all that. I kept trying to be like all the other boys in Oak Forest. I wore Beatle boots with cleats on the heels so I could make a clackety-clack noise as I walked down the halls. I bought the latest records—the Beatles, Herman's Hermits, the Monkees, the Supremes—so I could listen to them on my portable stereo. I played in the school band and went to solo competitions. I went to a music store in Oak Lawn where I picked out sheet music. I went on field trips with my classmates to the Museum of Science and Industry, the Field Museum, and the Art Institute. I walked the streets of Chicago as if I belonged there.

Just when I started to feel comfortable, though, something would happen to remind me that I was an impostor, as were my mother and father. We weren't city people at all. We were rubes, yokels, hillbillies, hicks.

My father thought he was a clotheshorse. He shopped for sport coats and dress slacks and had a particular fondness for tweed hats with fake bird feathers in the bands, the likes of which I never saw any of my friends' fathers wear. But then there were the olive-green work suits that he wore for every day, the sort he'd worn when he worked on the farm, the ones bought from Montgomery Ward, the ones with the shirt cuffs tattered from catching on the points of his hooks. He might look dressy for school events or church on Sunday, but really he was always that dirt farmer, and my mother was never far from the woman who'd cut baby pigs' teeth, milked cows, plucked and cut up chickens, crawled under combines to grease fittings, and slopped the hogs. No matter the suits she wore to school when she taught or the fact that she had appointments to get her hair done at the beauty parlor or the earrings she wore, the truth was that she would, come summer, go back to wearing plain cotton house dresses and washing her feet in a dishpan on the back steps after she finished mowing the yard at our farmhouse. And each summer, I would spend three months downstate, away from Oak Forest and my friends. I could never join them in Little League baseball. I never joined the scouts, never had a paper route. Come summer, I was a stranger, and each autumn I had to come back and be on the outside of everything that had happened while I'd been gone.

I remember what it felt like to come back to our duplex and to once again be a part of suburban living. After three months on our farm, where I spent many days working with my father or entertaining myself, I was eager for the ready friendship of my Oak Forest pals. Playmates were nearby, and there was always a pickup game of some sort to join. We played sandlot baseball. We shot baskets in driveways. We had football games on vacant lots. We rode our bicycles all over town, sometimes circling by girls' houses those years when girls were first starting to catch our eyes. We listened to the Silver Dollar Survey on WLS via transistor radios. We saved our allowance and bought records at Zayre. We went to picnics and birthday parties at the Yankee Woods forest preserve. We gathered at Tony's Corner Store or the Pick 'n Save to buy candy. We sat on the floor in one another's bedrooms and traded baseball cards. For me, an only child, such camaraderie was exhilarating.

But I also remember the awkwardness of easing myself back into my friends' company. Three months often set me apart from them, and in a way, it seemed as if I were the new kid again each autumn.

School started after Labor Day, and that weekend my parents and I made the five-hour drive north, our Chevy Belair loaded down with clothes, household goods, my Schwinn Sting-Ray bike, and the television set we transported back and forth each year. I remember arriving late in the afternoon and setting out on my bike to see who I could find.

I pedaled my bike down Debra Drive in one of the newer subdivisions where my friend Larry lived. I went to Larry's house and rang the bell. His mother answered. She was a thin red-haired woman who had a southern accent. She was wearing yellow pedal pushers and a sleeveless black blouse. She held the storm door open with her hip while she smoked a cigarette. She had her left arm slung across her stomach and her right arm propped on top of it at a right angle. Smoke curled from the cigarette—an extremely long cigarette, it seemed to me—which she held between her fingers.

"Larry's not here," she said to me in that drawl of hers. Her voice quavered just a bit. "He's across the street at Dale's."

I thanked her.

She took a drag from her cigarette and blew smoke out the side of her mouth. "So you're back," she said. "Back from downstate."

Yes, I told her. I was back.

She'd always seemed fragile to me, as if she were one loud noise—one slamming door, one alarm clock ringing—from coming apart. Larry's father was a tall broad-shouldered man with neatly combed hair. He was a businessman who wore suits and ties even around the house. He moved through the world with an ease and confidence that I envied. Next to him, his wife always seemed out of place. I was more like her, on edge, fearful that I'd be revealed as an impostor and be expelled from paradise.

She only sighed, but in that sigh, just before she let the storm door close, I sensed something I couldn't have articulated then, but now I wonder whether it contained everything she knew about what it was like to be far away from the place she'd once known as home, what it was like to be a stranger constantly having to prove that she belonged. At the time, I only wanted to find Larry and Dale and to slip back into the life I'd had to leave that summer.

I pushed my bike across the street, and I heard the thin sound of a transistor radio and then Dale's voice coming from behind the garage.

"Boss," he said with enthusiasm. A new way, I'd soon learn, of saying that something was neat, keen, cool.

Dale and Larry were sitting on the grass, listening to the radio.

"When did you get back?" Larry asked.

"Today, just now," I said. I plopped down on the grass with them. "Here I am."

Dale had his drumsticks and was tapping out a rhythm on the brick wall. He played snare drum in the school band. He was a stocky kid with sandy blond bangs that he was always swiping out of his eyes.

"Here it is; here it is," he said as he turned up the volume of the radio.

The song, one I'd never heard, was an instrumental—electric guitars with a driving drumbeat. It featured a wild drum solo three times during the fairly short song. Each time, Dale tapped it out on the bricks.

"Man, that's boss," he said when the song was done.

"What was that?" I asked.

Dale looked at me with amazement. "That's 'Wipe Out,'" he said.

"Everyone's listening to it," said Larry.

"*Every*one," said Dale. "It's boss, and you're not boss if you don't know 'Wipe Out.'"

Let me be clear that I was far from naive when it came to current music. I listened to the radio. All summer, on our farm, I'd listened to WJPS Tiger Beat Radio out of Evansville, Indiana. I knew the hits. I knew "Wild Thing" by the Troggs. I knew "Barbara Ann" by the Beach Boys. Heck, I even knew

"The Pied Piper" by Crispian St. Peters. But somehow that summer "Wipe Out" had escaped me.

Sitting there with Larry and Dale that day, I felt inadequate, as if "Wipe Out" were the kind of song only suburban Chicago boys would know—even though suburban Chicago boys were far from the California surf culture that had given rise to it. Still, they weren't as far away as it seemed I was on our farm, where I listened to the radio in my bedroom and gazed out the window at the fields that stretched on to the horizon.

"I'm cool," I said.

Dale laughed. He pointed a drumstick at me. "No one says cool anymore. Not if you're boss."

It seemed as if I'd always be trying to catch up with the lay of a land that shifted while I was gone each summer, trying to get hip to the new fashions, the new songs, the new things everyone had done while I'd been gone. Trying to be boss.

One night, my mother went to see the movie *My Fair Lady*. She went with a group of other teachers from her school. A girls' night out, she said, which seemed like an odd thing for my mother to say. I'd never known her to go out at night without my father. She'd let her driver's license lapse when we moved to Oak Forest, and she relied on him for transportation. He drove her to school and picked her up in the evening. He drove her to the Laundromat on Saturdays or to the Pick 'n Save to do our grocery shopping. He even drove her to PTA meetings and school events. That was his job, to get us where we needed to go.

But on this night, my mother was going somewhere without him. She was going out with the girls, which seemed like something Doris Day might say in one of her films. "I'm going out with the girls," she'd say, hooking her purse over her elbow and tugging on gloves that matched her wrap. "Don't wait up."

My mother didn't carry a purse. She carried a pocketbook. And she didn't wear a wrap. She wore a sensible wool coat, and in that pocketbook she had a plastic rain bonnet. She even had plastic rain booties to slip on over her oxford shoes. She was more Aunt Bee from *The Andy Griffith Show* than she was Doris Day. But here she was, about to have a girls' night out. She was going into the city to have dinner in a fine restaurant and then to see this movie that was, she assured us, all the rage.

Who was this woman? *All the rage?* Where had she picked up that bit of lingo?

When she came home, her coat smelled of cigarette smoke. I tried to imagine her in the restaurant at a table with women who smoked. I tried to imagine my meek Christian mother laughing at their jokes, contributing to their conversation, but no matter how much I tried, I couldn't quite manage it. My mother—the mother I knew so well—didn't fit into that picture. But I could tell, from the way she said she was off for a night out with the girls when she left and from the way she hummed "I Could Have Danced All Night" when she tidied up the kitchen and made ready for bed, that she wanted to be Eliza Doolittle, plucked from the lower class and transformed into a sophisticated lady.

I remembered the night my father asked her to open a bottle of champagne for supper and how the cork hit the overhead light and sent pieces of glass down onto our food. Even now, I remember how humiliated she was, how sheepish my father was, and how obvious it had been to me that much of the time we were posing—impostors, each of us.

When I was in middle school in Oak Forest, I played in a Saturday morning basketball league in addition to playing on the school team. My eighth-grade year, my coach was one of my teachers.

Mr. O'Connor was tall and slope-shouldered. His sport coats and suit jackets always seemed to be too short for his long arms. The knobs of his wrists stuck out from his cuffs. He was soft-spoken and genteel, and my father, of course, was not.

At the end of the basketball season, the coaches voted on which boy should receive the sportsmanship award. It was an award I wanted to win, but I ended up losing to another boy. Somehow—and I have no idea how—my father found out that I'd lost the award because Mr. O'Connor hadn't voted for me. At least, that's what my father claimed. I imagine now there was something about Mr. O'Connor that my father didn't like. Maybe it was his height. Maybe it was his good manners. Maybe it was the coats and ties he wore. Maybe it was everything that gave the impression that he'd had advantages other people—people like my father and mother and me—would never have.

Whatever the reasons, my father was carrying around a load of whoop-ass when he happened to encounter Mr. O'Connor one Saturday morning in front of the post office.

He asked him what the hell he thought he was doing voting for someone other than his own star player. My father reported the encounter with relish when he came home from uptown.

It was Saturday, and the day already felt strange to me since basketball season had ended. The last of the snow was melting, and the warmer air suggested that spring would soon be there. But instead of renewal, I sensed an end to things: winter, my middle school days, and, as I'd soon find out, my time in Oak Forest.

My father told his story as he sat at the dining table.

"I told him he was a damn fool. I asked him—didn't loyalty mean anything to him?"

He used his hook to pry his glasses from his face. They tumbled to the table with a clatter. His hooks were always marring something. He left scratches on doorknobs. He scraped the handles of hoes and shovels and rakes. He creased the corners of pages. He tattered the ends of his sleeves.

"Roy, be careful." My mother was sweeping the floor. Her voice was as soft as the broom bristles across the Linoleum. "You don't want to break your glasses."

"I told him. Don't you think I didn't." My father went on. "I said, 'Who do you think you are? You must think your shit don't stink.'"

My mother stopped sweeping. "Roy, you didn't."

"I sure as hell did."

Like my mother, I was mortified. I could just imagine what Mr. O'Connor thought about my father, and, by extension, me. Didn't my father see that his vulgar words and actions were merely reinforcing Mr. O'Connor's belief that he'd done the right thing by voting for someone else? How could the son of a man like my father be deserving of a sportsmanship award?

"And I told him another thing." My father banged his hooks together. "I told him he was lucky I didn't knock his goddamn teeth down his goddamn throat."

I don't know how I managed to face Mr. O'Connor when Monday came around and I went back to school, but I did, and he never said a word about the incident with my father because Mr. O'Connor was the sort of man my father wasn't, the sort who could control his emotions, who understood how to put an unpleasant encounter behind him and look toward the future with optimism.

My father could never let things go. So later that year, when the school board issued my mother a new contract along with a scolding—again, it was a question of discipline in her classes—he couldn't keep himself from confronting the president. Word had leaked out that he'd been in favor of asking for my mother's resignation, and my father wanted him to know he didn't like that, didn't like it one bit.

Mr. Rogers was a bald-headed man who wore glasses with black plastic frames. He wore short-sleeved white shirts and skinny dark ties held in place with a gold tie bar. His bald head was shiny. The fringes of dark hair were kept cut close and well groomed. He was, if nothing else, meticulous about his appearance and equally efficient with his work. He was exactly the sort of man my father had no use for.

I'm not sure where the confrontation took place nor the exact timing of it. As with the tongue-lashing my father gave Mr. O'Connor, his dustup with Mr. Rogers was something I never witnessed and only became aware of after the fact. As with all of my father's displays of temper, the aftermath left us with a certain degree of shame and feeling as if we were incapable of decent behavior. The run-in with Mr. O'Connor had its due and then faded. The one with Mr. Rogers was a different sort. It was the end of something, although at the time I didn't know the depth of that ending.

"I told him he was a son of a bitch," I heard my father say to my mother one night when I was supposed to be asleep.

"Roy, such language," my mother said.

"Honestly, Beulah. Did you expect me to keep my mouth shut? That bastard."

Despite the pain that my father often inflicted on me and the times he spoke sharply to my mother, he was always fiercely protective of us. Mr. Rogers had insulted my mother by doubting her ability as a teacher—by wanting her gone—and how was my father supposed to ignore that?

"It's late," my mother said. "We need to go to bed."

Later that year, my parents started talking about whether to stay in Oak Forest so I could go to a larger high school, where I'd have more advanced classes and more extracurricular opportunities, or whether to move back downstate.

One night that winter, my parents took me to the high school to register for classes, just in case we stayed, and then we started looking at houses in a new subdivision, again, just in case. For six years, we'd lived in our duplex. and I'd sometimes been ashamed when friends came to visit and realized that I didn't live in a house like they did. We were transients, and nothing announced that more than our duplex with a hide-a-bed in the living room and the other furniture we'd bought from secondhand stores. To look at these new homes, newer and finer homes, even, than the ones my friends lived in on Debra Drive, was to imagine a new life for us, one that would sever us from our downstate country life and make us suburbanites for good.

I won't assume to speak for my parents, who are both gone now, but I wonder whether, as we toured those new homes, they felt, as I did, that they didn't deserve them. These brick homes with two-car garages and paved driveways and gaslights in the front yards. The times we walked through them, as excited as I was to think that we might actually live in one, there was also a part of me that thought these were homes meant for other people and not for us. We were intended to live on the farm in a house that had no air conditioning or running water. A house we heated with fuel oil stoves that choked the air with fumes. A house where birds sometimes flew down the stovepipes and into our living room. A house where raccoons nested in the attic and at night scratched the plaster as they crept behind the walls. A house like that.

Then suddenly we stopped touring new homes. Somewhere, outside my hearing, my mother and father had been talking and they'd reached a decision. My mother resigned her teaching position, and at the end of the school year, we packed up what we wanted to keep from our six years in Oak Forest, and we moved back downstate.

Maybe in the end we just gave up. Maybe we surrendered to the truth of who we were and would always be, no matter how far I'd end up moving from the farm and the small towns of southeastern Illinois.

All I know is that as the school year came to a close, we made plans to leave Oak Forest behind us for good, to make one more drive south and never come back.

On graduation night, my mother took a Polaroid of me standing in our apartment with my diploma, but she didn't frame the photograph properly, so she cut off my head. I could be any boy in that picture. I could be Larry or Dale or Bob—any Oak Forest boy at all. But the one person I can never be is me.

Maybe we just wanted to go home.

Bastards

*I*nstead of remodeling the house on our farm outside Sumner, we took the hard road into town and started looking at houses there. We ended up keeping the farm, but we bought a house on West Locust Street from a man named John who lived next door to it, a man who had bought the house and upgraded it with the hopes of his older daughter and her husband living there, a plan that, for whatever reason, didn't work out. So now he was putting the house on the market, and my parents were interested.

John was a gentle sort, a man who owned a welding shop on the town's main street and spent summer evenings caring for his vegetable garden. He smoked a pipe and spoke with a lazy drawl. He was never in a hurry. I remember watching him stroll down the rows of his garden, stopping from time to time to pull a weed or gauge the ripeness of a tomato or pick a few ears of corn. When I think of him now, I think of the lazy creak of a screen door, the wafting smoke from his pipe, the way he'd start a sentence with, "Well, yes, sir, now you see . . ." He sold us our house for $10,000. When my father asked him what interest rate he was going to charge, he chuckled and said Uncle Sam would only get it anyway, so he wasn't expecting us to pay him any interest.

"I don't feel right about that," my father said, but no matter how much he insisted, John refused.

"You just keep that interest," he said. "I expect that'll be all right."

The house was a modest frame house with a front porch and clapboard siding—a well-kept home. John had laid new hardwood floors and had extended the kitchen at the back of the house.

"Now this is all right," my father said. "This is just fine."

He insisted on vigilance, and I can understand why, given his own carelessness that day in the cornfield. Our new house sat on a double lot. My father plowed the second lot and put in a large vegetable garden. He lined a row of peach saplings down the center of the backyard. We tilled and hoed and weeded. We watered and mowed and raked. My mother's flowerbeds were lush with peonies, zinnias, and marigolds. She planted iris bulbs, tulips, and daffodils. Our grass might have been full of clover, as most yards were, but we kept it mowed and trimmed.

A family was known by how well it took care of what it owned, my father said. On the farm, we could let things slip a bit if we got too busy to keep it all shipshape. There, our house sat at the end of a long lane and was invisible from the road.

"That won't fly in town," he said. "Here, people are always watching."

Evenings that summer, he walked through the backyard to check on the peach saplings and the garden. Then he sat on the front porch in a lawn chair and watched the night come on. In the twilight, he must have taken a last survey of our well-tended yard and felt the pride of having everything in order.

We were making a fresh start after those years in Chicagoland where our lives had felt odd to us. There, my father was no longer a farmer. He didn't work at all and had a hard time knowing what to do with his days. My mother was ill-suited for her life among people who were bolder and more assertive. I, on the other hand, started to think too much of myself. I entered my teenage years headstrong and ready to test my father's limits. We had raucous fights during which we shouted and swore and otherwise behaved like the heathens our neighbors below us in the duplex surely believed us to be.

"I'll take you down a notch or two," he often said.

We ended up in confrontations that sometimes turned physical. We shoved at each other. He whipped my legs with his belt. We screamed at each other. We said vile things.

"Mercy," my mother sometimes said. "Just listen to you."

My father and I often ended up in tears and then retreated to the stony silence of our shame.

That was what we were trying to put behind us when came back downstate. In our new house, though we never spoke of it, my father and I promised ourselves we'd be better.

We had a detached garage where he kept his Ford F-150 pickup truck. One night, someone let himself into the garage under the cover of darkness and walked out with some of my father's tools.

"Thieves," he said. He padlocked the garage doors. "Let 'em try to get in there now." He banged his hooks together. "The bastards," he said.

This all happened in the small town of Sumner, Illinois, population one thousand. A town of working class people in the southeastern part of the state. A town that prospered from the sweat of farmers like my father and oil field roughnecks and refinery workers and those who worked in the various factories in neighboring towns. We were blue-collar folks, and we knew the value of hard work and what it took to own something worth having.

We wanted to have kinder lives, and for a time in our new house, we did. Summer nights, my father and I sat at our kitchen table, listening to a Cardinals game on the radio. My mother popped corn and pared apples. We drank Pepsi-Colas and let ourselves imagine that such evenings could become our regular come and go.

My aunt and uncle and cousin paid us frequent visits. We had supper, and then we brought out the cards and played pitch, a bidding game that pitted a pair of partners against another pair. As we played, we engaged in good-humored teasing and taunting, and I reveled in the fact that my father and I could enjoy picking at each other the way family members did who didn't live in anger. A dig here or there surely wouldn't do any harm.

One night, I made a bonehead move and led with the king of hearts before the ace had been played. My father, who was partnered with my cousin, shook his head and said to him, "I can't believe that move. Can you, Phillip? Did someone just open the door and let Stupid walk in?"

Because he couldn't hold the cards in his hook, he kept them laid out and hidden behind the raised cover of a *Look* magazine. My aunt kept the magazine cover up so no one else could see them. He would tell her which card to play and she would put it on the table, but when I led that king of hearts, he used the point of his hook to slide out the ace and take the trick.

My uncle tried to ease the sting by saying, "That's just one trick. That's nothing to worry about at all. Let's see what the old man does now. Let's see if he's got the cards."

Maybe everything would have been all right if I'd said, *Yeah, old man. Show us what you've got.* But then my father looked at me, and he said, "You've got to pay attention. You've got to know what's been played and what hasn't. You don't see Phillip making any goofs like that. Now get with it, or no one will want you as his partner anymore."

My aunt said, "Oh, leave that boy alone." Her defense of me only called attention to my shame. "I'm sure he's doing the best he can. No need to ride him like that. After all, it's just a game."

But it wasn't just a game. It was another reminder of all that boiled between my father and me, all that we tried to keep locked up on nights like this when we were with people, all that bad blood. My face was hot. An ache came into my throat, and I choked back tears. I kept my head lowered and my eyes on my cards. I waited for the game to continue, but for what seemed like the longest time, it didn't. The clock on the wall hummed. The refrigerator's compressor kicked on. My uncle cleared his throat.

It became clear to me, then, that everyone was being cautious about what they said. My aunt and uncle and cousin knew my father's temper. They must have suspected that he and I were in the habit of knocking our heads together, and no one wanted to be the one to say the next thing, the thing that might cause us to explode.

Finally, my father returned to the game and pushed a card out into the center of the table. Even he could tell we were on the brink of something dangerous and was trying to get us back on safe ground. The one thing we shared was shame. I wish I hadn't been so sensitive. I wish he hadn't been so rough. I wish he'd shut down that power takeoff and made it impossible for his accident to happen. I wish he'd never had to put on those hooks and the anger that came with them. I wish he hadn't been so stupid in that cornfield. But I never said any of these things to him. I never told him that I was sorry for all that he suffered. We never talked about his accident. It was one more thing that we tried to contain and put away from us.

If it hadn't been for my mother that night around our kitchen table, who knows what might have happened.

What did she do? Nothing dramatic. She came into our kitchen and stood behind me. She laid her hand on my shoulder. She held it there, not saying a word, and finally my uncle played a card, and then my cousin, and then I did the same, and the game went on, and all the while my mother was there, her hand the lightest thing I could imagine at that moment, so light that I barely felt her touching me at all, but I knew she was, and that, as it would so many times thereafter, made all the difference.

"Who wants cake and ice cream?" she finally said, and like that, we went on.

Then one day my father noticed footprints in the snow around our house. It was winter—days of short light, icicles hanging from the eaves, snow on the ground. It was that snow cover that gave away the voyeur. We tracked his footprints around the perimeter of our house, a man who wore Red Wing boots. We could see the outline of the wing on the heels pressed down into the snow and the blurred letters of words we knew were "Red Wing Shoes." The man had walked around our house, turning at every window so he could look inside.

My father and I both owned Red Wing boots, as did a number of other boys and men in our town. I wore a size 10, my father a size 9. Whoever had left the prints in the snow wore a much larger size. How were we to ever know who it was?

"Well, it was someone," my father said, "and he better hope I never find out who he is."

On nights when I didn't have basketball practice—game nights—I came home after school and went to my room, where I stretched out on my bed, a quilt over me, and I read until my eyes grew heavy and the blue dusk began to deepen into night. I was alone in the house. In her retirement, my mother had taken a job at the local nursing home, where she worked as a housekeeper, cook, and laundress. My father was either doing something at our farm or loafing in the barber shop before making his way home.

The house was still. The only sounds were the roof joists popping as the sun went down and the frigid temperatures of night set in, and the wall furnace clicking on and off, the gas jets roaring to life. I made myself cozy in that silence. I didn't have to be on guard, worried over the next thing I might do or say to provoke my father. I was free to settle into a sound and peaceful sleep.

But now it gave me an eerie feeling to know that someone had stood at our windows and looked into our house. I hated thinking of what he must have seen—my fights with my father, my mother kneeling each night before bed to say a silent prayer, the times when my father called on me to help him with something—settle his eyeglasses on his face, hold a drinking glass so he could close his hook around it, unzip his pants so he could use the bathroom, zip them back up when he was done. Those were the things that were the hardest to imagine a stranger seeing, those private times when my mother was at work, and my father had needs only I could provide. His voice was shy when he made these requests. He became even more timid as he passed into his old age and on occasion I had to bathe him or clean him after he'd used the toilet. Our eyes would never meet, embarrassed as we both were. We'd be on the other side of our anger by then, but our language would still be the language of old foes, wary, reserved. The language of men who mistrusted our right to this love born from scars, considering it of questionable origin.

I wasn't sure I wanted my father to find out who was watching us. Part of me cringed to think of our privacy violated, but another part of me wondered whether the fact that someone was watching would keep us on the straight and narrow, make us kinder to each other. For several days running, no anger rose up between us. I came home from basketball practice to the supper my mother had kept warm for me, and as I ate, my father sat at the table with me, and we talked in normal tones about how the team was playing, the games that were coming up, how I was doing in school. My father had always taken an interest in my athletics and my schoolwork, but now there was no criticism in what he had to offer, no "You can do better." We were just a father and a son chatting on a winter's night, and when I'd finished my supper, I went to my room to do my homework and then later came out to watch television. My mother and father watched, too, and we were just a family like that, finally switching out our lights and lying down to sleep.

Then one night, the movie *In Cold Blood* was on television. I sat in front of our black-and-white Zenith set, totally immersed in the world of 1950s rural Kansas and the story of the murder of the Clutters on a November night in 1959. They'd been a family—a mother and father and a boy and a girl. They'd been living their lives without a thought that something like this might happen. The mother belonged to the local garden club; the father was a successful farmer. The girl was busy with her boyfriend the way girls are at that age; the boy played on his high school basketball team just like me. The depiction of the killers moving through the dark house set me on edge, and when they bound and gagged the Clutters and then shot them one by one, I felt that this was all too real, as it had been, of course, on that November night when Perry Smith and Dick Hickock, and not the actors Robert Blake and Scott Wilson who portrayed them, had committed those brutal killings.

I went to bed that night unable to close my eyes, afraid to go to sleep. I kept seeing the Clutters, hands and feet tied with rope, tape over their mouths. I kept hearing the shotgun blasts. Then I thought I saw a shadow move across my bedroom curtains. I imagined I heard the squeak of boots on snow. I even swore I heard a faint tapping on the glass.

Who was out there, or was it anyone at all? I was too afraid to lift the edge of the curtain so I could look outside. I didn't sleep at all that night, one of the longest nights of my life, and in the morning there were no fresh prints in the snow.

But something had changed for me. Even now, it's hard for me to say what it was. Something about what it cost to live in fear, to live with the prospect of violence, to always be on guard against it. Some knowledge of all that my father gave up when he had his accident, the joy and ease that came from living in the present moment, no thought about what haunted him from the past, no dread of what might be waiting ahead of him. That's what I'd inherited from him, this unsteady hold on life, this mistrust, this suspicion. Something about watching *In Cold Blood* and then later imagining someone at my bedroom window had made me understand what I'd long felt but always lacked words to call by name. I was imprisoned, locked up inside my father's rage, held in a place I didn't want to be, but I didn't know how to escape.

Then one night our back door opened. My father and I were in the living room with the television on, but we heard the door, and we both turned toward the kitchen where my mother was finishing the dishes.

I heard her turn off the water at the sink, and I knew she was gathering up the hem of her apron so she could dry her hands as I'd seen her do so many times. I heard footsteps on the linoleum floor, heavy steps I knew didn't belong to my mother but to whoever it was who had opened our door and stepped inside—a man from the sound of those steps, a man who was wearing heavy work boots.

I heard my mother's measured voice. "What is it that you want?"

My father was already pushing himself up from his chair, the evening paper he'd been reading sliding to the floor.

I felt the cold air about my legs, and I knew the intruder had left the back door standing open.

"We don't have anything you want," my mother said, her voice rising just a bit. "Are you lost?"

Her question pierced me. *Yes,* I wanted to call out. *Yes, I'm lost.*

But I didn't, of course. I got up from my chair. I followed my father into the kitchen. I followed him toward whatever danger might be waiting there.

The intruder was a boy, a tall, skinny boy with a CPO jacket too short for his long arms. The knobs of his wrists were blanched white from the cold. His face was red and inflamed with acne. He wore a pair of Red Wing boots with stains—oil? blood?—darkening the toes. His wild eyes darted about, first to my mother, then to my father, then over my father's shoulder to me.

"Are you lost?" my mother said again. She actually took a step toward him. "Are you looking for another house?"

The boy swallowed. His Adam's apple slid up and down his gullet. He held his mouth open, and his thin lips quivered. His long blond hair was in tangles. He had an ugly gash in the meat of his left hand. He tried to stanch the blood by wrapping his palm in the hem of his coat.

"Are you hurt?" my mother said. "Let me see."

She reached out her hand to him, and the boy looked at that hand that was veined and wrinkled and chafed raw from the detergents in the laundry at the nursing home. The boy lifted his eyes and looked at my mother with what I knew was yearning, the same desire for her refuge and protection that I had often felt, the same desire to finally be unburdened. I didn't know this boy or what his trouble was, but I knew what it was to want to be free from this life that pressed down on me, this bastard life, a life that was spurious and counterfeit, a poor imitation of the happier one that might have been mine if my father hadn't made a mistake that day in the cornfield, if he hadn't lost his hands and become an angry man.

The boy let his hand come free from the hem of his coat. He studied the cut. Then he looked at my mother again, and in my silence I urged him to go to her, to let her take care of him. I wanted to watch her clean his wound, put ointment on it, bandage it. I wanted her to speak to him in her soft tones, to tell him, *It's fine. It's fine; everything will be just fine.*

The rest of my life was out there waiting for me. I wanted it to be a life of goodness. I wanted to look back at this moment someday and to be able to say it made all the difference.

But I can't say that because just as the boy was about to reach his cut hand out to my mother, my father banged his hooks together.

"Who the hell do you think you are," he said, "to come into my house?"

That's when the boy got spooked. He turned and ran, his boots loud on our floor. He ran out into the cold night, and I felt my heart go with him. I felt something leave our house, some measure of hope. If there had been more room for my mother's kindness that night, there might have been a healing, one that might have saved me.

"You better run," my father said.

It would take me years and years to escape the anger of that house, and even now, when I live a more gentle life, I still feel like I'm fighting the rage my father left inside me, always trying to tamp it down, always on guard against its return.

I'd lock it up if I could, forget the combination, and let the tumblers go to rust, so no one could ever turn them.

"That poor boy," my mother said that night.

I'll always wonder what drew him to our house. Was there a mercy there that my father and I were too blind to see? Was it ours for the claiming, if only we would? Maybe we were too busy feeling hurt to see that we could forgive ourselves; in spite of my mother's influence, we couldn't accept that we, the damaged and the maimed, had a right to a kinder way of living.

My father closed the door that night. He fit the curve of his hook to the underside of the knob and pulled until the door was latched. He opened his hook and concentrated on grasping the tab of the lock inside the knob. He didn't ask for help, and neither my mother nor I offered it. It took him awhile, but he kept working at it until, finally, the door was locked.

"That kid was wild," my father said. "He was out of his head." He banged his hooks together again. "To come into our house? What kind of person would do that? What's happened to people? What kind of life does that kid have?"

"He was in trouble," my mother said.

Something in her voice shook me—a note of weariness, a resignation. It was as if she were giving up on my father and me, and maybe she did for that brief moment. Maybe she thought, *God, help them.*

I could tell my father heard the same thing I did. My mother, the eternal believer. His face crumpled with confusion. Had he heard what he thought he did? This was the woman he'd married when he was nearly forty, the woman who'd loved him before the accident and beyond, the woman he'd counted on for so much. When he finally spoke, his voice quavered. "I know he was," he said. That was as close as he could come to telling my mother he was sorry for all the anger he'd brought into our home. I was ashamed of my own part in that anger. I was ashamed of the two of us.

Although I stayed in the kitchen, some part of me went with my father as he moved on into the living room. I heard his hook scraping at the doorknob as he locked it, closing us in, sealing us up.

"You don't have to worry now," he said. In his bluster, I heard what I'd never been able to distinguish in the noise of all our fighting. He was proud. He was watching out for us. This was his secret. His world was always tilting. He was on guard. Let the bastards come. He'd be ready. Wounded as he was, he knew no other way to speak of love.

—ᴍ—

Once upon a Time

One evening the next summer, the story of the boy who came through our back door already receding behind us, I came home after being out with some friends and found my mother and father entertaining a visit from an elderly couple, Otis and Mabel. Their daughter was one of my father's childhood friends, and Oat was now one of the elders at the Church of Christ we'd begun to attend. He was a slack-faced man with pouches of skin hanging under his eyes. He was tall and soft-spoken, and he smoked a pipe with a silver stem. Mabel was a trim woman who had her gray hair waved and set each week—a small woman who laughed easily, throwing up her hands in delight. They were kind people who wore their faith lightly. I always felt comfortable around them, and their presence in our home didn't unsettle me as would have been the case had certain other people from the church, more proudly pious, been the ones sitting on our couch when I opened the door and stepped inside. Seeing Oat and Mabel was more like seeing a favorite uncle and aunt.

It was sometime after the wheat harvest, a midsummer time when my father and I didn't work until dark on our farm. I'd been with my friends at a dirt track we'd built in a vacant lot at the edge of our small town, a track for racing our bicycles. After the racing, we'd sampled some Red Man chewing tobacco one of my friends had taken from his father, and after deciding it wasn't to my liking, I headed home.

There was still plenty of daylight left when I came inside our house and found Oat and Mabel visiting with my parents. An oscillating fan sat on a table by the window in the living room. Each time it turned toward the coffee table in front of the couch, it lifted the corner of a *Life* magazine cover, and a few pages stirred before settling back down. Mabel smoothed the magazine cover with her hand.

"Where you been?" my father asked me.

I could have told the truth, that I'd been at the bike track, racing, but instead I was more cryptic. Maybe it was because I didn't want him to find out about the Red Man. I had something to hide, so I let my response get all loosey-goosey.

"Just screwing around," I said, and then I went on to my room.

I don't recall whether I listened to record albums or whether I read or exactly what I did. I only know that once Oat and Mabel were gone, I was in trouble.

My father called me from my room into our kitchen, and he asked me what I thought I was doing, using that vulgar language in the company of such decent and devout folks.

"'Screwing around,'" he said with disgust. "What kind of thing is that to say?"

Of course, I'd heard him use much worse language, but in the presence of Mabel and Oat, people he genuinely liked and respected, he was on his best behavior. My own language, mild as it may have been, embarrassed him. I don't remember whether I pointed out his hypocrisy to him, but I easily could have. Whether I did or I didn't, it quickly became clear to me that my father's character wasn't under consideration. I was the one being called to account. Even my mother, who had always been tolerant of my missteps and poor decisions, was looking at me with disapproval. Our kitchen felt oppressive at this moment when my parents were letting me know how much I'd disappointed them. My father sat at the chrome-edged dinette table, his jaw muscles working the way they always did when he was angry. My mother stood facing me, her hands on her hips.

"Lee, you're better than language like that," she said.

"It's just a word." I tried a feeble defense. "It doesn't mean anything."

"It most certainly *does* mean something," my father said, "and don't act like you don't know what."

Yes, I knew the sexual connotation of the word, but I also knew in my heart of hearts that I hadn't been using it in that sense when I'd answered my father's question about what I'd been doing. I also knew, as I stood there before my parents, that no matter what I'd meant when I'd said "screwing around," I'd been wrong to say it.

"Is it a word you think either Mabel or Oat would use?" my mother asked in her soft voice. When she was done, she pressed her lips together in a tight line. I didn't answer. I merely bowed my head to indicate my agreement that I'd been wrong. She said, "Then you shouldn't use it around them. Do you understand?"

"I do," I said, and it was true; I really did.

In retrospect, it seems that our move back downstate brought upright men and kind living into our lives. My father was friends with John, and the barber, Tubby, who listened patiently to my father's stories and sent him home with new jokes to tell, and Harold from across the street, who snaked out our sewer line when it needed it, and the other Harold at the garage, who came to the rescue one Saturday night when we were down in the country and the solenoid on our Oldsmobile went out and left us stranded.

Good men, each of them.

I, in the meantime, found myself slipping into trouble. I was rebellious, roaming the streets at night with my friends to see what mischief we might find. I ended up in places I shouldn't have been—a closed pool hall for a private showing of stag films, riding in cars with men who would eventually end up in prison—and did things outside the law. We broke into the high school. We stole things from stores. We set fires. I was trouble and also troubled. I drank until I passed out. I said vile things to my father and had physical altercations with him. I was, in short, an embarrassment to my parents.

I can only forgive myself when I decide to imagine how my mother and father, once they'd gotten beyond the shock of my mother's pregnancy, must have delighted in my birth. I have to go back to the days in our farmhouse, those days when we first became a family.

Before I could read, my grandma Martin taught me rhymes. She said them over and over until I could say them too. She couldn't see to read, and I didn't know how. Memory and recitation, though, required no clear eyesight, no reading skills.

I'd lie in bed with her and listen to her say,

Ding-dong, bell,
Pussy's in the well.
Who put her in?
Little Johnny Flynn.
Who pulled her out?
Little Tommy Stout.

Or,

Georgie Porgie, pudding and pie,
Kissed the girls and made them cry.

One of my favorites, just for the sound it made, and for its pure silliness, was the one in which my grandma said, "What's your name?" And I answered, "Puddin' Tane. Ask me again, and I'll tell you the same." I knew what pudding was, and the fact that a little boy could be named that delighted me. What Tane was, I had no idea, but the rhyme was one I loved to say, and I said it with gusto—so much so that my grandma and my parents stopped asking me for my name. I suppose I was getting on their nerves. No problem. I just asked myself, so I could have the joy of answering.

Sometimes my grandma sang to me. She sang, "Yankee Doodle," and "She'll Be Coming 'Round the Mountain," and "Old Dan Tucker." I loved to sing, and I had a beautiful voice that I kept until puberty when a bullfrog seemed to take up residence in my throat, and everything I tried to sing ended up being sharp or flat, or both.

Neither of my parents had any talent for singing—couldn't carry a tune if they had it in a bucket. But I had a talent for it, and I had a knack, I started to learn, for all things verbal.

When I started first grade, I went to that two-room school in Lukin Township just a few miles east of our farm. I rode a yellow bus and learned the stops at the neighboring farms along the way. Groups of children—brothers and sisters—waited at the ends of their lanes. They got on the bus, often squabbling over something, pushing at one another and calling one another names until the driver, Mr. Kirts, told them to pipe down and behave. He was a patient man, but he brooked no mischief. When he told you to settle down, it was like he was a kindly uncle calling you to task for being a nuisance. "Aw, Henry," someone might say. At his urging, we called him Henry. "Aw, Henry." A sheepish hang of the head, an embarrassed tone, maybe a stubbing of a rubber-capped sneaker toe against the metal leg of a bus seat. "We were just messing around."

I didn't understand the give-and-take between brothers and sisters because I didn't have any. When I was with others who did, I often felt like a person who was "it" in a game of tag, watching the activity around me, running hard to try to touch someone, listening to the laughter and the squeals of those I had to chase. It was like they all knew something that I didn't just by virtue of the fact that there were more of them. Not only were there more, but they shared the same house. They knew things about being with people that were hard for me to learn. I didn't have to share my toys with anyone. Most of the time I didn't even have a playmate. I knew nothing about the attachment of siblings—that bond that could spin them out of being annoyed with one another into a fierce love in a heartbeat.

Thinking back on it now, I suppose I also had a talent for observation. I watched closely, trying to figure out what it meant to have a family. I spent a good part of my childhood in the midst of the middle-aged, the elderly, the childless, the infirm. By the time I was five, my mother was fifty and my father was forty-eight. When we visited their friends and relatives, there was only rarely another child around. All the children had grown and left those homes. On occasion, grandchildren might be present—sometimes distant cousins—and I always felt like a needy child when an adult would give me a gentle nudge and say, "Go on. Go out and play."

Joining those groups of kids was excruciating for a shy only child like me. Although I secretly wanted to, I often shook my head and said, "No, thank you," preferring to stay close to my mother and father. I spent countless afternoons and evenings sitting in kitchens and living rooms, or on front porches or out in backyards, listening to people tell stories.

I fell in love with the structure of a good story. That once-upon-a-time. That element of something unknown, something to discover. That march of people through time and space. That feeling of satisfaction that came from finally knowing the answer to that universal question, "What's going to happen?" In a good story, the answer always came as a surprise; the unexpected

rose to the surface, and when it did, I saw the world and its people in a way
I never had.

But a good story had music too. Its sounds could delight the ear. It had verse.
Consider the turns of phrase I heard:

"He ate that fish like a starving fat kid."
"I told him I didn't chew my cabbage twice."
"I cabbaged onto that fish and wouldn't let it go to save my life."
"'Mister,' I said, 'you're breeding a scab on your ass.'"

The music of simile and metaphor and the unexpected verb.

I heard the same on television. Cartoons like Foghorn Leghorn, and his
good ol' boy southern accent, gave me colorful ways of playing with language. "That's a joke, ah say, that's a joke, son." As did Huckleberry Hound,
the laconic blue dog who said things like, "And stuff like that thar" and sang
an off-key and inaccurate version of "Oh My Darling, Clementine." Or Fred
Flintstone with his "Yabba dabba doo!"

The music of language was all around me, even in the sounds of the coun-
tryside: the three-note call of the whip-poor-will from the woods at night;
the two sharp notes of the bobwhite, evenly spaced and rising in pitch; the
bass lowing of the cows; the chirping of the spring peepers at our pond; the
echo that came back to me at dusk when I stood in our farmyard and
shouted my name.

Who was I, this child my father at first didn't want, this only child, this
shy child, this boy blessed with words?

I was the boy the teacher regularly chose to read the captions for the film
strips we watched at school.

"Good," she always said. "Very, very good."

I wanted to be good. So much of the time, my father made me feel like I was
a disappointment. Although he could be proud of me—"Show Dewey how
you can dribble that basketball," he said one night—there was more often
the sharp word, the lash of a belt, the look of disapproval when I couldn't do
a chore to his satisfaction. "You want me to make you a sugar tit?" he asked
me whenever I started to whine. "Can't never did nothing. Try it again."

It pleased me, then, to hear those words of praise from my teacher. I loved
the gold stars she put on my spelling lessons. I loved the way she gave me

featured roles in the little plays we did for the holidays. I loved the way she said, "Does anyone other than Lee know the answer?" when I kept raising my hand to respond to her questions.

One day, I sat with my mother, and she opened my *Fun with Dick and Jane* reader on her lap.

"Do you know this word?" she asked me.

"Run," I told her.

"That's right."

It was late afternoon, and the sun was streaming into our kitchen. The cat clock on the wall wagged its long black tail. The refrigerator hummed. Moisture beaded up on the enamel water bucket we kept on the counter. I'd helped my mother fill it at the pump behind the house that morning before I left for school. Now we were sitting at the kitchen table, and my mother was pointing to another word.

"I don't know that one," I said.

"You will," she told me. She closed the book very carefully and ran her hand over the cover. We were alone. My grandmother was napping in her bedroom. My father was out at the machine shed. My mother's voice was very soft, even more so than usual. She said to me, "You'll learn to read all the words in this book, and then you'll learn to read even more." She handed the book to me. "You'll see," she said.

And like that, I saw the letters of the word I hadn't known. "See!" I said.

"Yes," my mother said. She put her arms around me and hugged me to her chest. "Yes."

I have no children of my own, so I can only imagine what she must have been feeling at that moment—pride in this boy whose world, though he didn't know it, was already starting to change. A world that was larger than our eighty acres. Those gravel roads led to the hard road and on to the state highways and interstates. And books led to all sorts of places—places that filled my imagination and gave me permission to dream of a life that wouldn't involve our farm, our small town, our history of disappointment, the one that started the day my father found out my mother was pregnant and said to Doc Stoll, "Can you get rid of it?"

Though it would be easy to imagine that the word *verse* was far removed from my father, its roots actually bind us together. The Latin word *vertere* means "to turn," and the Latin word *versus* refers to a turning of the plow, a furrow. My father spent years turning over those eighty acres in furrows, straight and true. I've written line after line, turning at the right margin to start another one. I've loved the labor of words just as my father loved the labor of the land. Farmer, writer—both of us doing our work.

"Once upon a time," I say now, and just like that, I'm back in our farmhouse, an only child with the whole day—a whole life—ahead of me.

After breakfast, I sit on the living room floor and play with my Lincoln Logs, thinking about the fairy tales my mother reads to me and how so many of them begin with a step back in time—there was a poor woodcutter and his wife and his two children; a sweet little maid, much beloved by everybody; a man and his wife who had long wished for a child, but in vain. I love a good story and the way it begins at a point where anything is possible. I'm often left to entertain myself, and as a result I learn to live inside my imagination.

School has let out for the Christmas holiday. Outside, snow drifts in our lane and falls over our barn lot, where my father scatters hay for our cows. Soon he'll take an ax to the pond and chop away the ice so they can get to water. I don't think a thing about what it takes for him to be out in the cold and snow doing these chores. I'm six years old, and I'm intent on building a cabin. I love the way the logs lock into place, every notch squared, every piece fitting together. The logs pile up until I can put on the slanted roof.

So much of the life that I live in our real house is ragged and uncertain because my father is an angry man. I watch television and read storybooks and build cabins with my Lincoln Logs to keep myself from thinking about what might happen if I say or do the wrong thing. I dream of other places, other lives.

Soon I go into the kitchen, where my mother is ironing clothes. She keeps a bowl of water on her ironing board. She dips her hand into the bowl and then sprinkles droplets across one of my father's twill work shirts. She doesn't have a steam iron, so she relies on the curve of her wrist, the graceful shake of her hand, to dampen the cloth and make the wrinkles easier to straighten.

I ask her to play a game with me. She says, "Can't you see I'm busy?"

Then, because she's a good mother, she says that one day, come summer, she'll play with me all day long. She promises.

She spends her days giving her attention to the children in her class, children I envy because I don't like sharing her with them. I love her because she's kind, and a little shy like me. She's different from my father, who will take off his belt or pick up a yardstick and whip me on my legs when I don't behave or when I do something that displeases him.

My mother never spanks me. She makes strawberry-preserve-and-butter sandwiches when I ask for a snack, or graham crackers with vanilla icing between them. She bakes gingerbread cakes and whips real cream. We have no air conditioning, so she sits beside my bed on hot summer nights, stirring the air by waving a *Look* magazine over me until I fall asleep.

My mother's hair is gray. I don't know how old she is. I only know she's older than my friends' mothers. As time goes on, I'll learn that she was forty-five when she had me. I'll know that my conception was unplanned. After my father is dead and I'm a man close to thirty, she'll tell me that the first thing he said to the doctor on learning of her pregnancy was, "Can you get rid of it?"

When I'm six, my life sometimes feels like that, like I wasn't meant to come along, like I'm a stranger in our home, a foundling taken in by this aging couple. I hold on to what's familiar. My mother's hair is gray, and she has a set of metal clips that she sometimes uses to set a wave. I know where to find them in her dresser drawer. The clips have sharp teeth that hurt when I close one around my finger.

Each morning, my father slips his stumps into the holsters of his hooks, and my mother helps him settle into the harness of canvas straps that he wears across his back. Thick rubber bands wrap around the base of each hook. A tension cable connects to a lever and runs up the holster. When my father extends his arms, the muscles in his shoulders draw on the cable, and the pincers open. The number of rubber bands determines the degree of tension. I'll learn all of this later.

When I'm six, the hooks are mysterious. When my father lies down for a nap, my mother drapes them by their harness over a straight-backed chair. Sometimes I slip my slender arms down into the holsters and try to make the hooks open. Sometimes I pry the pincers open with my fingers, careful not to let the hooks snap closed and pinch me between them.

I'm too young to draw a line of cause and effect from my father's accident to his anger. I only know he has no hands. He can't hit fly balls to me the way my friends' fathers do. He can't shoot baskets. He can't throw a football. He manages, though, to grasp his belt or a yardstick when I misbehave, and in spite of that, I love him because he's my father whether he wants to be or not.

"You're just talking to hear yourself roar," he says to me when I'm rattling on about this or that.

He says it when we're in the living room, and I'm trying to tell him about my Lincoln Logs. "I built this cabin today. A big cabin. A cabin that used every log I had. That big."

My father is worn out from his chores. His face is red from the cold. The legs of his overalls are wet from the snow. He's forty-eight, and he has a son he never meant to have. A son who's often oversensitive—some would call him delicate. "A pantywaist," my father sometimes says. "Don't be such a pantywaist." A son that requires energy that he simply doesn't have. A son he can't touch.

"Tell your mother about it," he says.

"I did," I tell him. "She said this summer we'd have a day when she plays with me all day long."

He says it again: "Talking to hear yourself roar."

I let myself hate him just a little because I understand now: he's just called me a liar.

He goes into our woods and cuts down a cedar tree. It fits into a stand in our living room. I help my mother hang icicles from its branches. We decorate the tree with lights and ornaments—shiny balls and bells and stars.

I decide I want to have a party, a Christmas party. I've seen people have parties on television. I love watching shows like *Leave It to Beaver, I Love Lucy, The Donna Reed Show*. I know how parties work. You set a date and ask people to come. They show up looking nice and happy. Everyone has good things to eat and drink. They play games. Sometimes there's music, and then the people dance.

"I want to have a party," I tell my mother. "Tonight. Start calling people."

"Who should I call?" she says, the tremor of a grin twitching at the corner of her mouth. I don't register the fact that she finds this amusing and is trying her best not to laugh.

"Everyone," I say. "We're going to have a party."

I'm determined. I keep pulling Christmas decorations from the cardboard box where my mother keeps them. I am a boy who wants what he wants. I hold a string of silver beads in my hand.

Finally, my mother stops me. She explains that a party can't just come together in a whipstitch. People have busy lives; they need more than a few hours' notice. "And what would I offer them?" she asks. "I don't have time to prepare anything."

I won't hear of it. "We're having a party," I say again, my voice rising, the tears starting, a tantrum about to break.

My father is suddenly there. "Just keep it up, Mister, and I'll give you something to cry about."

I curl up on the sofa, still clutching the beads. This is the sofa that folds out into a bed. It's where I sleep. Now I turn my face to the sofa's back. I hear my father's belt buckle come undone, and I try my best to stop crying.

"Roy," my mother says, and then the two of them go into the kitchen, leaving me alone in the living room.

Soon the light grows dim, and I know that the afternoon is lengthening toward evening. *We're having a party*, I keep telling myself, and at some point, I fall asleep.

When I wake, the room is dark except for the lights on the Christmas tree. My mother has taken the beads. She's covered me with a quilt. In the glow of the Christmas lights, I can make out the familiar furnishings of our living room. The Philco television in one corner, the desk in another, the overstuffed chair by the window, the rocking chair near the end of the sofa, the oil heating stove along the wall. It's a room unlike any I've seen on television. No winding staircase to a second floor, no grand piano, no built-in bookshelves. I wake to the small room of our modest farmhouse. I try to imagine it filled with partygoers like the ones I've seen in my shows, but of course I can't manage it. I can't imagine the farm women wearing pearl necklaces, their husbands in snazzy suits and neckties. There are the people on television, and then there are people like us: farm people, people worn down by the hours of worry and work, people like my father who tried to unclog a shucking box without first shutting down the power take-off, people like my mother who never planned on having a son in the middle of her life and at a time when she has to do so much for my father. They have no time for the fantasies and tantrums of little boys like me.

I go into the kitchen, where my mother is putting supper on the table—a square oaken table made smaller by the absence of the two leaves in the middle. An oil-cloth-covered table just large enough for the three of us.

"We were going to have a party," I say.

My father is sitting at the table. He taps the place to his left where I always sit. The point of his hook makes a knocking noise.

"Honey, sit down," he says. "It's time to eat."

My mother says, "Goodness, I bet you're hungry."

What can I do but pull out my chair and sit? "We were going to have a party," I say again in a whisper. "Now it's too late."

At bedtime, my mother helps my father take off his hooks. They're in the bedroom. I'm lying on the sleeper sofa in the living room. I'm supposed to be asleep, but I'm not. I hear the points of the hooks scrape the floor as my mother drapes the harness over a chair. I hear her mumbled voice, and I know she's unpinning the white cotton arm socks that my father wears over his stumps. She's taking the safety pins from his T-shirt sleeves. She holds each opened pin between her teeth as she moves on to the next. Soon the light goes out in their room, and I hear the bedsprings creak as my parents settle down beneath the covers.

I call for my mother.

"What's wrong?" she says.

"I can't sleep."

This has been my habit ever since my parents bought the sleeper sofa for me and got rid of the crib where I used to sleep at the foot of their bed. I call for my mother, and she comes and sits beside me until I finally nod off.

My father's patience is wearing thin. He says, "Do you want to be a baby all your life?"

"I'm not a baby," I say.

"Then hush up and go to sleep."

"I'm not a baby," I say to myself. "I'm not."

I wait. "Mom?" I say again.

She comes to me then, and she tells me I have to learn to fall asleep by myself. She says, "Just close your eyes and count your blessings. Think of all the good things from your day."

My Lincoln Logs, my mother's hair clip, the string of silver beads, the Christmas tree. Its cedar smell is all around me. It smells like somewhere else, like somewhere I might go one day.

I have no way of knowing that this scent, years and years in the future, will always take me home, will leave me standing on the porch of that farmhouse, knocking on the door, knowing that once upon a time there was a family here, wishing for just a few hours more with my parents, wanting to tell them how sorry I am that I once hoped that my mother might be young and pretty and my father might have hands he'd use to ruffle my hair while he called me sport or buddy or pal.

Fifty-eight years have gone by since the day I'm recalling. I'm older than my parents were then. I have no children of my own. Sometimes I wake from dreams in which I'm knocking on the door of our farmhouse, even though it long ago went to ruin. My voice is small and afraid. I say, "Mom? Dad?" I say, "Don't you know me?" I say, "Please, won't you let me come in?"

I close my eyes and I can almost hear them. If only they'll open that door, throw their arms around me, I'll be able to say, "There we lived long and happily. We went cheerfully home and came to no harm. There was all care at the end, and we lived in great joy together."

Instead, I'm a little boy knocking on a door that no longer exists anywhere in the real world. I listen; I wait. I knock again.

My Lost Year

*D*uring my teenage years, I remember my father coming home in the evening, excited to share a new joke he'd heard while loafing at the barber shop.

"Wait until you hear this one," he said one night, already starting to chuckle in anticipation of the punch line. He was sitting at the supper table with my mother and me. "Marvin was playing eighteen holes with his friend, George."

The truth is, even though he became an angry man after his accident, my father loved people. He sought out their company whenever he could.

"Let's go for a drive," he might say on a Sunday afternoon, and off we'd go, over country roads, stopping here or there just to sit awhile and visit with folks.

Summer evenings, when he went out to check on our garden before supper, my mother would start to wonder what had become of him.

"Go look for your father," she'd say to me.

I'd find him talking to our neighbor, John, both of them leaning on a post of the wire fence that separated our properties.

"Mom says supper's ready," I'd say.

"Tell her I'll be there," he'd say, and fifteen or thirty or forty-five minutes later, he would be.

He was a talker. "Sadly enough"—to return to his joke—"George had a heart attack and died on the eighth hole. 'How awful,' Marvin's wife said when he told her the story. 'Oh, you have no idea,' he said. 'The rest of the game, it was hit the ball, drag George, hit the ball, drag George.'"

How my father loved to make people laugh.

I discovered that I had a talent for mimicry. I liked to watch variety shows like those of Jack Benny, Red Skelton, and Flip Wilson. I imitated the characters they played. I could do Jack's frustrated cry, "Now cut that out!" I could even do his droll look, my elbow propped on my crossed arm, my hand to my cheek. And Red gave me a number of characters and bits: Freddie the Freeloader; Clem Kadiddlehopper; Deadeye; and the seagulls, Gertrude and Heathcliff. I memorized the catchphrases; I mimicked the voices. I used a falsetto to do Flip's Geraldine: "The devil made me do it." I also had two comedy albums that I played over and over, Bill Cosby's *To Russell, My Brother, Whom I Slept With,* and the Smothers Brothers' *Mom Always Liked You Best!* I memorized the routines and did them for my friends at school during lunch.

Somehow in the midst of all the ugliness that filled our home, laughter survived.

My mother was the shy one, the studious one, but even she, from time to time, could cackle and get absolutely silly over something that tickled her.

One night, she laughed so hard over something my uncle said, she had to take off her glasses and wipe the tears from her eyes. Her sisters, Gladys and Anna, had been the cutups. My mother, the oldest, had been a child of duty. She'd taken care of the younger ones—there had been three boys to go with the three girls—and she'd delayed marriage until she was forty-one, living with my grandparents, working in their general store after the school day was done, doing what she could for her family. She provided. She sacrificed. It saddens me sometimes to think she may have done this at the expense of giving full expression to the person she was. Perhaps she never even knew that person fully because she was too busy thinking of others. Still, there were glimpses of who she might have been without the burden of her obligations—that woman who could laugh until she cried. I have photos of my aunts striking silly poses. They were women who laughed easily. I have only a few pictures of my mother genuinely smiling. Most of the time, her lips are pressed together. I can tell she's trying to smile, but she comes across looking peeved. The night my father told the joke about Marvin and

George, she laughed. Oh how she laughed, and I can tell you, it was a glorious thing to behold.

I remember her more often, though, in moments of thoughtful solitude. On the rare occasions when my father didn't require her help and I was content to be by myself—when all her work was done—she liked to work a crossword puzzle or read a book or spend a few moments in silent prayer. I remember Sunday afternoons in our house in Sumner when she'd go into our living room with the newspapers, sit in her comfortable chair, and put her feet up on the ottoman. If it were summer, an oscillating fan would be running, its gentle sweep stirring the pages she held in front of her face. If it were winter, the heat from the wall furnace warmed her.

Eventually, I'd hear the paper slide to the floor, and I'd find my mother had nodded off. What a moment of grace it must have been for her, those afternoons when no one demanded her attention, when all she had to do was rest. I wish the rest of her life had been like this. I wish she hadn't had to work so hard or suffer so much loss. She was a good and kind person, and she deserved better.

Those days in Sumner—my teenage years—I found myself inching away from her, my dear mother, who'd shown me everything there was to know about loving people. I was stupid, then, in the way only young people can be: selfish and lost inside a self I didn't even know, completely blind to those like my mother who would have done anything to save me.

Like most teenagers, I was busy trying on identities. My freshman year of high school, I walked the straight and narrow. I was a good student, a basketball player, my natural inclination to shyness more pronounced by virtue of my status as a new kid in school. After those six years in Oak Forest, I suddenly found myself in the midst of boys and girls who'd known one another all their lives. I was the one who'd have to try to fit in.

From what I could gather, the men in our small town—and by extension the boys who wanted to become those men—valued cars, hunting and fishing, sports, trucks, camping, motorcycles, mechanics, brawn, pitching washers or horseshoes, bird dogs, beagle dogs, fried catfish, fried tenderloin, fried anything, Marlboro cigarettes, Seagram's 7 whiskey, professional wrestling, Pabst Blue Ribbon beer. Not much room for an appreciation of what I'd always loved: reading and writing.

One day when I was in health class, there was a knock on the door. Our teacher, Mr. Baker, answered it. From where I sat, I couldn't see who was outside in the hall. It was a sunny, drowsy day in late autumn, and I was trying hard to concentrate on learning the 206 bones in the human body. We were focusing on the skull that day: occipital, parietal, frontal, temporal, sphenoid, ethmoid. I guess you could say I was deep inside my own head, and I was startled to find Mr. Baker calling my name. Whoever was in the hall wanted to talk to me.

Oh, it's bad when someone interrupts a class to call you out into the hall. The other students perk up, their curiosity aroused. Their first assumption is that you're in trouble. It was my first assumption that day as well. Either that or something horrible had happened in my family and someone had come to give me the bad news.

The man in the hall was the band director, Mr. Cavaliere. He was a tall man with thinning hair and a soft belly. He was young, probably still in his twenties, and he had lips that one might have called full or pouty if they wanted to be complimentary, or puffy or fat if the intent was less than kind. The boys in our school called him Pussy Lips.

"You're Lee?" He closed the door to my classroom. "Lee Martin?"

In situations like this, I was soft-spoken like my mother. "Yes," I said, and he had to ask me to repeat myself, as people often did in those days. "I'm Lee," I said, this time a little louder. I could hear Mr. Baker droning on behind the closed door. He'd moved on to the facial bones: nasal, lacrimal, palatine, maxillae.

Mr. Cavaliere pulled at his lips as he studied me. "Mrs. Richardson recommended you."

Mrs. Richardson was my English teacher. She was a stern woman who didn't suffer fools. To have her recommendation, even if I didn't yet know for what, made me feel good about myself.

Mr. Cavaliere said, "I need someone to be the narrator for our Christmas production of *The Nutcracker*."

"A narrator?" I said.

Already, I was afraid. To speak in front of a gymnasium filled with people? That was something quite different from reading the film strip captions down in Lukin at that two-room school.

"You'd be offstage," Mr. Cavaliere said, "with a microphone, and you'd have passages to read. Mrs. Richardson said you'd do a good job."

I had no doubt that I would. I knew how to read. I knew how to project my voice when I needed to. I wanted to make Mrs. Richardson proud of me. I wanted to earn her respect. But here was this man, an effeminate man with that horrible nickname, and I couldn't imagine telling the other boys why he'd come looking for me—boys who would never understand why I was narrating a ballet.

"Afraid I can't," I said.

"Excuse me?" said Mr. Cavaliere.

"School work," I said. "Basketball practice." I mumbled something about not having time.

I was relieved when Mr. Cavaliere didn't press me. All he said was, "I'm sorry to hear that." Perhaps he was a man who was accustomed to people turning him down. He pulled at his lips again. "Mrs. Richardson spoke so highly of you."

The truth was, I was sorry, too—sorry I'd let down Mrs. Richardson, sorry I'd disappointed Mr. Cavaliere. I didn't really know him, but he seemed to be a very nice man. Most of all, though, I was sorry for myself. I still am. I still think about that moment outside that classroom when I kept myself from doing what I really wanted to do, when I refused my talents.

Looking back at it now, I imagine that was the moment when I began to drift. By the end of the school year, I'd be trying on a new identity. I'd become a hood, a juvenile delinquent, a punk. I'd be that way through the summer and on through my entire sophomore year. My lost year, as I've come to think of it.

"I don't know what's been troubling you," Mr. Miller, my algebra teacher and the assistant basketball coach wrote to me on my final exam. I squeaked by with a D. Me, the honor student, who'd always made As and Bs in school. "But I hope you get it figured out over the summer and get back to being the boy you used to be."

That was a sobering message. It told me how people were starting to think of me. I knew I was on the wrong path, but I couldn't stop myself.

I had a group of friends who liked to roam the streets at night looking for mischief. We broke into people's garages to steal the beer they kept there. We broke into the high school and spent the dark hours stacking people's lockers, drinking Cokes in the teachers' lounge, and always, always, always looking for something that we could steal. We stole cigarettes from a neighborhood market. We traveled to nearby towns, riding along with someone's parents, to steal record albums, paperback books, and whatever caught our fancy. This was a time, the early '70s, when hairspray for men was popular. "The wet head is dead," a commercial for the Dry Look by Gillett told us. One Saturday, I stole a can from a drug store on Main Street in nearby Olney. Earlier that day, I'd stolen the *Woodstock* album from Whittaker's Stereo on Whittle Avenue by slipping it inside my jacket. Record albums gave me pleasure, and though I always had enough money to pay for what I stole, I liked the thrill of getting away with something. In my home, my father was strict. A child of the Depression, he hated waste and would snap at me if I left a light on in a room I'd vacated.

"You think money grows on trees?" he'd say to me.

He was strict about his expectations. He insisted I get good grades, do well on the basketball court, have good work habits. When basketball season was over and I no longer had to keep my hair short, we fought constantly over its length.

"You want to look like a girl?" he'd say.

He expected me to dress a certain way, look a certain way, behave a certain way.

Each thing I stole, even that can of hairspray, was a big fuck you to him and his expectations.

My sophomore year was my year of rebellion. For the most part, my home was an unhappy place, fraught with the tensions between my father and me. Beneath its tidy appearance, it was a place of sadness. I remember so many nights when my mother would come to my room to tell me good night. She'd be in her long white nightgown, rubbing lotion into her hands, a weary look on her face. I knew I was a burden to her: my derelict behavior, my sinking grades, my foul mouth, my rage. Those nights, she looked at me as if I were someone she didn't know. She must have wondered what had happened to her shy son, to her good boy—the one who'd sat on her lap while she read him a story; the one who clung to her skirts, afraid to turn his face to the world; the one who called for her when he woke in the night; the one she prayed for now.

"Count your blessings," she always told me the nights I had trouble falling asleep.

I imagine that when she went to her own bed, she lay down and stayed awake a long time worrying about me, wondering what would happen to this son who'd come to her in the middle of her life.

All my life, I'd been a sleepwalker. My mother told me that when we lived on the farm, she sometimes found me roaming around the yard. She started putting straight-backed chairs from the kitchen around my bed at night, so if I tried to get up, I'd hit them and wake myself.

"It was too dangerous to have you walking outside in your sleep. Mercy, who knows what might have happened."

So she did what she could to save me. She put those chairs around my bed.

I was still sleepwalking when I was fifteen, but I only had my parents' word for it. I never remembered a thing—never recalled getting out of bed, never knew I'd moved through our house with the stealth of an intruder. I'd read about Charles Manson and how he sent members of his "family" out at night to break into homes. While the occupants slept, Manson's disciples moved furniture around, a calling card to let the homeowners know someone had been in their house. Manson called these night-time raids "creepy-crawling." I imagined the terror the homeowners must have felt those mornings when they came from their bedrooms to find tables where only the night before chairs had been, to see everything they thought was theirs changed, to know that while they slept, someone had come inside and done this. Though my own "creepy-crawling" was involuntary and harmless, I imagine it must have startled my mother. There were times when my fights with my father got so intense—shouting and shoving—that I sometimes said vile things I didn't mean but couldn't help saying, so great was the pressure that built up when I butted heads with him.

"I'll kill you," I'd scream, and somewhere along the line, he started to believe it.

"He's out of his head," he said to my mother once. "There's no telling what he might do."

Was this thought in her mind when she woke one night and saw a light on in our kitchen? Did her heartbeat quicken when she passed my bedroom and saw I wasn't there? Did she walk into the kitchen, afraid of what she might find?

"What are you doing?" she asked me.

The refrigerator door was open. I was standing at the counter with my back toward her. She must have taken a few steps toward me, enough so she could see what I had in my hand. A milk carton.

"I'm having a glass of milk," I said.

When she told me all this the next morning, she reported that I said this in a flat, low voice, one devoid of emotion, one that must have been chilling.

"You looked at me," she said, "but I could tell you didn't know I was there. It was like you were all alone. It was the saddest thing."

She said I drank the milk and then walked out of the kitchen and went back to bed, leaving her to close the milk carton and put it back in the refrigerator, to clean the glass and leave it in the drainer, to turn off the light.

Her house must have seemed peculiar to her then, this troubled place violated by strangers. My father and I were a dangerous mix. My sweet, gentle mother didn't deserve the upset we brought her, and to this day, I regret the ugliness I forced her to witness. Although I didn't know it then, we were close to turning into gossip. Because of me, we were about to give up ownership of our story. We were about to let it be the town's to narrate.

I was seeing a girl then, an eighth grader. Her name was Amy, and she was a tiny thing. I spent most Saturday evenings at her house on Cary Street. My friends often came along. It was that kind of young teen relationship—hanging out with friends, holding hands, exchanging love notes. Then there were the times when we'd find ourselves alone, and I'd put my arm around her and she'd lay her head on my shoulder and brush her eyelids against my throat. "Butterfly kisses," she called them. We had that sweetness of innocent love that maybe only the young can have, and we had it at a time when so much of my life was anything but innocent. It wasn't a love that would last, but at the time, it was everything to me. When I was with Amy, I felt closer to the boy I'd always known, the one I was close to losing forever—the boy who at one time had moved through the world without hurting anyone.

Our small school housed grades K–12. Mornings, before the last bell, I'd be with Amy outside her classroom. We'd be in the hall, holding hands. One morning, her teacher, Mr. Cockrum, came by and told us to "break those hands." Odie Cockrum was old school, a narrow-faced man with a sharp nose. It was 1970, and he didn't tolerate public displays of affection. I only mention him because he becomes an important player in what happened next.

Apparently, he kept some money in the drawer of his desk, money that went missing.

"He asked me if you stole it," Amy said to me one morning.

We were standing outside her classroom as usual. She was holding a paperback copy of Erich Segal's *Love Story*. Many of the girls in our school were reading it that year. The movie starring Ali McGraw and Ryan O'Neal was in the theaters. I'd read the book, which wasn't a thing I wanted anyone to know. It wasn't the kind of book boys in our school normally read. Instead, we passed around books like the 1748 erotic novel *Memoirs of a Woman of Pleasure*, a book everyone knew as *Fanny Hill*. But I'd read *Love Story* because when had I ever been able to resist a good story, plus at heart I was a romantic. So I stole the book from Piper's Sundries and gave it a read, and I'll admit I cried when Jenny died after telling Oliver that "love means never having to say you're sorry." Years later, I'd read that Erich Segal patterned Oliver not after Al Gore, as Mr. Gore claimed, but actually Gore's roommate, the actor, Tommy Lee Jones, whom Segal described as "a sensitive stud with the heart of a poet." When I was fifteen, that's exactly what I wanted to be—and I want it still, to tell the truth. The problem, then, was that any sign of sensitivity was taken as a sign of weakness. So I stole the book and read it in private.

"Why does he think I stole it?" I asked Amy.

She shrugged. "He just does."

"What did you tell him?"

"I told him you didn't do it."

Bless her for her steadfast faith. Bless her for being, at the age of thirteen when her mother was telling her I was trouble, the one who believed in the best part of me.

That afternoon, the principal, Mr. Weber, called me to his office. He was a big man who wore short-sleeved white shirts whose buttoned collars cut into his fat neck. The boys in our school called him Wimpy after the character in the Popeye cartoons who loved hamburgers. They called him Wimpy or, worse, Hog Jowls. He sat behind his desk and rested his hands, fingers interlaced, on top of his mounded stomach. I sat in a chair across the desk from him and waited for the accusation I knew was soon to come.

"Mr. Cockrum is missing some money," Mr. Weber said. He looked at me for a long time. I sat there in silence. I knew he was trying to crack me. He was waiting for me to confess, but the truth was I had nothing to tell him. I hadn't stolen the money. Finally, he said, "This will all be a lot easier if you just return the money."

"I don't have it," I said.

He leaned forward, his hands now pressed into his desk. "You spent it. You know I could call the police."

"I never had it. I didn't steal it. I'm not guilty of anything."

He looked at me a long time, his brow furrowed, his eyes boring into mine. Finally, he said, "We have our eye on you." Then he told me to go back to class.

In a few days, Mr. Cockrum would find the money in a filing cabinet, forgetting that he had put it there himself. No one ever apologized to me. I'd become the boy who wasn't worthy of an apology because it was common knowledge that he was up to no good. I was the boy that everyone had their eye on.

OK then, I remember thinking. *If that's the boy people like Mr. Cockrum and Mr. Weber think I am, then I'll be that boy, and I'll never say I'm sorry.*

It was around this time that I decided to run away from home. It was a harebrained scheme, one that I foisted on two of my friends. I'd had enough. I was leaving.

The plan started to take shape in my head one Sunday afternoon when I had another fight with my father. I've long forgotten our point of contention, but I still recall the way I felt when I stormed out of the house: abandoned, forsaken, as if indeed Doc Stoll had done what my father requested and had gotten "rid of it."

There were many times during my teenage years when I felt orphaned—times when my mother's love wasn't enough to counteract the ugliness with my father—but there was something about this particular Sunday that left me more wretched and woebegone than ever. Next door, the Murrays were coming home from church. Their daughter, Patti, was demure with her long straight hair, sleek and brown, and a modest shift dress whose hem hit her at her knees. She was a kind, soft-spoken girl, perhaps shier even than I. She was a good girl, and I could imagine how proud her parents must have been of her. Across the street, I heard a piano being played. The Moans, I knew, were gathering around it, and sure enough, just then, their voices rose in unison, singing "What a Friend We Have in Jesus."

That was a song that always made me sad. I know it's supposed to be a song of consolation, a hymn about taking our troubles to Jesus in prayer so he can relieve us of them, and from time to time, I tried. I asked him to ease the troubles between my father and me. I asked him to help me not to be such a bad boy. I asked him for peace.

It never quite worked, to tell you the truth, and it wouldn't work that Sunday when I walked past houses and saw people being families: pitching horseshoes in the backyard, laughing on porches, piling into the family car for an afternoon drive. Sure, I knew that everyone had their troubles—I knew that the woman who lived catty-corner across the street from us was an alcoholic and that my friend at the end of the street had his own miseries with his stern and reclusive father and that another friend didn't know who his father was—but on that day I felt like a pariah left to roam the streets with my own sorrow.

I stopped at the small market on the next street over. A widow named Wanda owned the store, a hardworking woman with a hard-drinking son, and I'm ashamed to say I stole from her, this woman who was never anything but nice to me, as she was on this Sunday when I asked her if I could use her phone.

"Long as it's a local call," she said in her loud, pleasant voice. Somehow, despite the burden of her own circumstances—it was clear that she was barely getting by—she managed to be cheerful.

"Yes, it's local," I said.

"Go on, then." She bent her head toward the phone, which was on the wall behind the counter. "I got canned goods to dust," she said, and then she moved out from behind the counter and disappeared down an aisle with her feather duster.

Looking back on it now, I imagine she gave herself this chore just so she could let me have my privacy. She was a good woman, and if she were still alive, I'd tell her how sorry I am that I stole from her. I'd even give her money to pay for all the cigarettes and Hostess snack cakes and candy bars and bottles of pop that walked out of her store underneath my coat.

I called my friend Steve.

"I've had it," I told him. "I'm leaving."

He was the happy-go-lucky sort. He liked rock music, NASCAR, and Johnny Carson. He was also vain about his appearance, favoring sandals and jeans and old army shirts with the sleeves cut out. He'd finally let his curly hair grow out and picked it into an Afro. The racist insults he got—those calls of "Nigger Knots" when he walked down the halls at school—didn't seem to bother him at all. He was usually singing softly to himself—Jethro Tull's "Aqualung," Steppenwolf's "Magic Carpet Ride," Led Zeppelin's "Whole Lotta Love"—and was oblivious to the nastiness around him. I was drawn to his buoyancy. He was a great sidekick, like Carson's Ed McMahon, quick to laugh and never taking offense. What he liked about me, I don't know. I only know he was a fine companion, always upbeat and eager to please.

I told him about the fight with my father. I'm pretty sure I said something clichéd like "He doesn't understand me." I seem to recall that I even went as far as to claim that my dear mother didn't understand me either. "I'm not going back," I said.

There was a silence on Steve's end of the line. I could hear a television on in the background. Finally, he laughed. "That's crazy, man. Where you going to go?"

I thought he'd understand. I thought he'd say, "I'll go with you." I didn't know how to respond.

Finally, he said, "Really, man, you don't want to do that."

Now, he was serious. I think he may have even been a little bit afraid. He knew what I, immersed in my misery, couldn't see clearly. To leave home at the age of fifteen would be a stupid thing to do, the sort of mistake I might never be able to correct. It might ruin me.

He tried to reason with me. He said to hang in there, things would get better. I could hear the urgency in his voice. I knew how hard he was trying to convince me.

But all I said was, "I thought you were my friend."

"I am," he said, and now, of course, I see he was doing what a good friend should have done, trying his best to keep me from doing something foolish, something I'd surely regret.

But on that day I felt betrayed. "I'm going," I said, and I hung up the phone and walked out of that store, uncertain what my next steps would be.

I walked down Cary Street toward the southern edge of town, where the houses became fewer in number until finally a grassy lane led back into woodlands. I walked past Amy's house. She and I were on the outs. She had, for whatever reason, broken up with me. "She gave you the mitten," my father said, using an old-fashioned idiom that made no sense to me. It was what he always said with great delight when a girl rejected me, as if he took pleasure in suggesting that no one would ever love me.

So there I was, my girl gone, my best friend a traitor, my father a torment—just a few steps away from a country song. I felt, as the song on the television show *Hee Haw* said, "Gloom, despair, and agony on me." On the show, they always played it for laughs—four men in bib overalls, drinking from jugs and singing about their misery, all of them breaking down in tears at the end—but out there that Sunday afternoon, I couldn't find anything to laugh about. I just kept walking until I was deep in the woods, and the only sounds were the birds and the squirrels chattering above me in the trees.

I stretched out on the ground, my head resting on a fallen log, and I stayed there, not wanting to go home but not knowing where else I might go. I'd long had a fantasy of jumping a freight car and riding it to wherever it was going. In fact, I'd written a few scripts for what I thought would be a good television show, a show about a drifter who did just that. Every episode began and ended with Bob Dylan's "Like a Rolling Stone" playing over my character's arrival or departure. But I'd never thought far enough ahead to what it would take to actually jump a freight car—where and how and when. I lived in my head a lot in those days. I had grand and romantic desires but not much practical sense. I was writing and creating. My parents had gotten me a Smith Corona portable typewriter—a manual—for me to practice on when I was in my typing class. My mother had gone to my teacher, Mrs. Shan, and asked her what model of typewriter she would recommend. I love my mother for doing that, for noticing my talents and doing what she could to encourage them. My father, as far as I know, never balked at the money for the gift. He didn't try to stand in my mother's way, as he had when I was a little boy and he hid my book from the children's book club, intending to send it back. He put out the money for that typewriter, and I loved him for that; I suppose I even loved him that day when I lay in the woods wanting to do anything but to go back to my home.

Then I saw the snake, a long black snake slithering through the dead leaves, steadily coming straight toward me.

That's what made me get up. That's why I walked out of the woods and kept walking until I was home. At least, that's what I told myself. The truth was I went home because Steve had been right. Where else did I have to go?

My father had driven down to our farm, my mother said. She was reading the Sunday papers. I went to my room and tried to do some homework. I stayed there until my father came home and my mother called me to supper. We sat at our table and ate, and we were shy around one another as we always were after a fight.

Then, for some reason—maybe it was the uncomfortable silence, or maybe it was just my natural inclination to be the peacemaker—I said something I'd never said to my father. I said, "I love you."

He looked as if I'd hit him. His face crumpled and then twisted into a face of anguish, and I could tell he was close to crying. I knew I'd embarrassed him—made him feel, perhaps, that he wasn't worthy of my love.

"You don't have to say that," he finally said.

I didn't know what else to do. I told him I was sorry.

For a while, I tried to keep my mind on the things that gave me pleasure—the books I loved to read, the stories I liked to write, my English class. I tried my best to tell myself that I wasn't the ne'er-do-well others thought I was. I had a vision of what I wanted my life to look like. I loved the old Dick Van Dyke show. He was a writer, a television writer, and he spent his days with typewriter and pen. He had a nice modern home in the suburbs. He had a good kid and a beautiful and faithful wife. He was witty and urbane, the sort that made friends easily. He was who I wanted to be.

But I was years away from being able to move that easily through the world. For the most part, I was brooding and shy and somber and reserved. "If you ever smile," a classmate wrote in my yearbook, "I'll crack up." It wasn't that I lacked a sense of humor or wanted to be a loner. Deep in my heart, I loved people. I just had to get to know them before I could decide if I could trust them enough to let them know the sides of me I usually kept hidden. Like my father, I was always on guard. Disaster was just around the corner. Someone, or something, was waiting to hurt me. This was what my father had given me, this suspicion, this mistrust.

When I think back to that time in my life—the year I've come to call my lost year—I believe I can see all that threatened me, all that lured me away from the boy I'd been. First, there was the desire to fit in when I was the new kid downstate. I remember so well the first time I was with one of the Moan boys when he broke into Wanda's garage beside her store so we could steal the beer her alcoholic son kept hidden there. Then there was the resentment that had built up inside me from living in a house of anger—a resentment that found its expression in behaviors I knew my parents wouldn't approve of. Above all, though, was the feeling that I wasn't worthy of love. Despite my mother's goodness, and the way she always told me that my father loved me, otherwise he wouldn't get so angry with me, I could never quite shake the feeling I'd had that Sunday when I'd told Steve I was leaving—that feeling of being unwanted, of not having a single place on earth where I truly belonged.

Is it any wonder, then, that I considered trading in my idea of a Dick Van Dyke life—happy and stable—for the life of a vagabond? If I felt like a pariah so much of the time, why not just hit the road?

That Sunday had been a trial run, the first time I'd said it out loud—*I'm leaving*—but it had set a spark beneath my heels, one that would continue to burn.

Nights in my room, I lay on my bed and listened to music. Canned Heat invited me to go up the country to someplace I'd never been. I loved the lyric from Bob Dylan's "Don't Think Twice, It's All Right," the one about walking a lonesome road with no idea of a destination, and of course there was "Like a Rolling Stone" and its question of how it would feel to be without a home.

I fantasized about a different life. Little by little, a plan began to take shape. It was ludicrous in all of its details, because after all I was a fifteen-year-old boy who didn't know squat about the way the world worked. But in my mind, it was glorious. I'd go north. I'd return to the place where once everyone had known me as a good boy. I'd left a girlfriend, my first, behind in Oak Forest. We still wrote each other letters from time to time. In the aftermath of Amy's refusal, I couldn't imagine anything better than being with Beth again.

She was a cheerleader with short sandy hair and a winning smile. Her nickname was Toots, and as the name suggests, she was full of spunk and good spirit. She was the sort you'd want on your side when things were tough. She was the first girl I kissed. Our hearts broke when I moved away.

"Try not to be so weird all the time," she wrote in my yearbook, "and you'll be fine. Love Forever, Beth."

We knew, at the point she wrote this, that I was moving back downstate. We promised to write and visit each other once we turned sixteen and could drive. Then there I was, a sophomore and not quite sixteen, but I was tired of waiting. I needed to be with Beth. I needed her to keep me from being "so weird." I was never sure what she'd meant by that—I thought I was a pretty regular guy—but I trusted her to know what was weird and what wasn't, and I thought I was at a place where I could use her common sense, particularly when I didn't seem to have any.

My mother had an old phone book from Oak Forest on the shelf above the deep freeze in our kitchen. One afternoon, when I was alone in the house, I took down that phone book and tore the pages from it that I decided I might need: listings of apartment complexes from the yellow pages, places I might get a job. I decided the Pick 'n Save grocery store might be a good bet. Didn't they always need someone to bag groceries and stock shelves? I figured I could do that. I thought I'd live with Beth and her parents, or maybe my best friend Larry and his family, until I could get on my feet and rent my own place. In my fantasy world, I had nary a thought of how in the world it would be possible that Beth's or Larry's parents would allow such a thing. I just thought I'd be visiting for a while, and wouldn't that be the truth? I had $200 in a savings account at the bank. It would be a good idea to take that to stake me on my adventure.

And how would it begin? How would I make the 238-mile journey to the north? I had no car, no driver's license. As much as I liked to fantasize about hopping a freight train, I really wasn't sure how to go about it or how I would know if the train was going anywhere near Oak Forest.

I had another friend named Ricky. He was the first boy to grow long hair in our school—hair down to his shoulders—and he suffered endless ridicule. One day in our homeroom before the first bell sounded, another boy—a jock—took a pair of scissors, sneaked up behind him at the front of the room, and cut out a hunk of hair. I remember how Ricky turned slowly, how the jock held the blond hair in his hand, laughing. The taunts had been merciless: "Do you squat when you piss, Ricky? Do you wear your mother's clothes? How much for a blow job?"

Ricky stared at the jock with what I can only call a restrained heat. He was calm. He was deliberate. He raised his right arm and used his fingers to tuck his hair behind his ear. He did the same with his left. Then, with no sign of emotion whatsoever, he said, "It'll grow back."

He turned and walked to his seat, leaving the jock still laughing, but with less enthusiasm by the second, still holding a pair of scissors and that hunk of hair, coming to realize—at least I hope if he didn't then, he did somewhere in the years ahead—that he looked like an idiot, like a coward, like a little boy lashing out because he was afraid.

Ricky was a hanger-on in my small group of friends. He always sought our company; we never sought his. Some evenings, he'd appear at my door, and I'd let him sit with me in my bedroom and talk about music as I played albums. Other times, he'd show up on the streets when we were out on Friday or Saturday nights, and we'd let him stay with us until the time came when he had to meet his stepfather who would be waiting for him uptown to take him home.

He lived in the country a few miles east of town. His stepfather was the postmaster. What had happened to his biological father, I don't know. I only know that his stepfather seemed to be a decent man who was well respected. His mother appeared to be hardened by whatever turns her life had taken, and maybe, at least from my limited perspective, just a bit erratic and fly-by-night.

Ricky was on his own most of the time, wandering, and I imagine, looking for a place to land, looking for people who would welcome him. Like anyone who was somewhat different in a small town, he had trouble fitting in. When he came to us, we obliged. After all, he was smart, and he was funny, and he liked music, and he was inventive. He had ideas. Granted, most of them seem a bit stupid in retrospect, like the time he dried celery leaves and rolled them in Zig-Zag papers, promising us "a smooth smoke." But still, he was always thinking of something, and he was eager to please us.

He was particularly eager to please me, and though I have no right to speculate, I wonder now whether he had a crush on me. If so, he was doomed to suffer an unrequited love because my own romantic interests were focused solely and energetically on girls.

Still, one moment sticks in my mind. We were camping out in the woods near the railroad trestle behind my house—Steve and I and a couple of other boys we sometimes hung out with. We hadn't invited Ricky, but somehow he found us. He sat with us around our campfire late into the night when we were settling down into our sleeping bags.

He kept saying, "I ought to be going." But he never did. "I'm going to be in deep shit with my old lady now," he finally said. "I might as well stay."

"You don't have a sleeping bag," I said.

He shrugged. "No sweat. I'll be fine."

And with that he stretched out on the ground, his hands behind his head. He was perpendicular to where I lay, so we made a T. My head was a few inches from his leg. Usually I brought a pillow with me on these campouts, but for some reason, I'd forgot to grab one before I left home earlier that evening. I was having trouble getting comfortable on the hard ground, and somehow in my tossing and turning, my head ended up touching Ricky's leg for just an instant.

"Sorry," I said, and quickly moved my head back to the ground.

"It's OK," he whispered. "I don't mind."

I took him at his word. I lay my head on his leg with no thought at all of the affection that may have been behind his offer. I only knew that I was comfortable.

And now, as I think back to that night, *comfort* is the word that comes to me. Ricky offered me a kindness, and though it may have been self-serving, that thought didn't occur to me at the time. Then, it was simply one boy doing a kindness for another.

The other boys were asleep, and I started to tell my plan for running away to Ricky. We spoke in whispers. I told him about my fights with my father. I told him I wanted to chuck it all and go to Oak Forest, but I wasn't quite sure how I'd get there.

"Drop out of school?" he said.

"The hell with it," I told him.

"Don't you have to be sixteen to drop out?"

We were quiet for a while, thinking about that fact. I wouldn't be sixteen for another six months.

"I can't wait that long," I finally said. "My parents would never let me anyway. I might as well go."

"Can I come along?"

"Why would you want to do that?"

"You know." We were now coconspirators. "What's there to keep me here? I'm just a freak. Like you said, the hell with it."

"You're really smart." I was trying to talk him out of coming along, not because I didn't want him to go but because I genuinely didn't want him to take a chance on ruining his future. "You don't want to mess anything up."

I realized I was also trying to talk myself out of leaving.

Then Ricky said, "I'll steal my mother's car. We'll leave in the middle of the night. We'll make it easy. No sweat."

I went to sleep that night dreaming of Oak Forest. I woke once and saw that the campfire had burned out. Embers glowed in the ashes. A breeze moved through the canopy of the woods. Some sort of wild animal—deer? raccoon?—rustled through the brush on the other side of the creek. My head was still on Ricky's leg. I felt him shift his weight, and I lifted my head and turned to look at him.

He sat up. "I'm cold," he said. He had on a short-sleeved shirt, the tails hanging out. "I'm going."

"Going where?"

"Home. I'm cold. Been shivering for a while now."

He hesitated, one hand on the ground, preparing to push himself to his feet. Now, I wonder whether he was waiting for me to offer to share my sleeping bag, but at the time I had no thought of that. I felt bad that he'd been shivering while I'd been sleeping, warm and cozy, inside my sleeping bag, but what could I do about that? I could have unzipped the bag all the way, and the two of us could have lain under it, but that wasn't something I wanted to do.

"I knew you'd get cold." I didn't mean to scold him, but I imagine he may have thought I was. "Why didn't you just get up and go?"

He ducked his head and his long hair hid his face. He used his fingers to tuck that hair behind his ears.

"I didn't want to wake you," he said, and without another word, he got to his feet and made his way through the woods to the gravel road that would take him to town and then home, where I knew there would be hell for him to pay.

Now I think of him lying there in the cold, shivering, wanting to get himself somewhere warm but not able to bring himself to leave, perhaps choosing to linger in the pleasure of my head on his thigh. I haven't known anything about him for years and years, but I wonder whether his life was kind to him. The last I heard he had a psychotic breakdown from dropping too much acid, and his beautiful mind was never the same. I wonder whether he remembers this night, the night he offered me such kindness. "I'll steal my mother's car," he said. "We'll leave in the middle of the night."

Mischief Afoot

I sat in my first class after lunch—Spanish—not listening to Señora Polston because I was going over all that was about to happen that night. In my head, I was already gone. I was far, far from that classroom, that school, that town. I'd spent the days after the campout getting everything in place. I'd even convinced Steve to come along. Maybe he felt guilty for trying to talk me out of it that Sunday afternoon when I called him to say I was leaving, or maybe—and I think this is more likely—he thought it might be a hoot. At any rate, he said he was in.

"Solid," he said, and put on his Foster Grant aviator sunglasses, the ones he'd found somewhere.

He was always finding things: cigarette lighters, a pick for his Afro, a stiletto knife. He was lucky that way. With him along, I felt sure we'd have a smooth ride.

Ricky stayed true to his word. He'd steal his mother's car at midnight and drive it into town. He'd stop at Steve's house to get him, and they'd drive to my house. Steve would come to my bedroom window and tell me it was time. I'd have my sleeping bag and a few clothes. We'd be on our way.

I'd been practicing. Nights, after my parents were asleep, I'd get out of bed, creep to the door, and open it. I'd take special care with the screen door that creaked, opening it as slowly as I could before stepping out into the night. I'd stand there in my front yard, imagining the night, coming closer all the time, when I'd finally be free from my father.

Those last days, I felt bad about what this would all do to my mother. I told myself I'd explain it all to her one day. I'd tell her I couldn't bear the anger between my father and me. I couldn't stand to bring such ugliness to her life. Such was my logic when I was fifteen. I was tired of seeing how much my mother suffered because my father and I couldn't find a way to get along. Better to go. Go and explain later. Just go and give my mother some peace.

I'd watched her breaking down—those rashes on her hands from the laundry detergent at the nursing home; a few days when she lost the vision in her left eye, something about her optic nerve, which I, in the typical fashion of the self-centered boy I was, never took the time to understand; the stoop of her back getting more pronounced, the burden of being my mother pulling her to the ground.

She was sixty years old at the time. My constant fear, as an only child of older parents, was that they might die while I was still young. I particularly feared my mother's death because I couldn't face the prospect of being left alone with my father, but there I was, willing to leave both of them. I couldn't have said this then, but now I imagine I was leaving, in part, because I couldn't bear to disappoint my mother any longer, and that's what I was afraid I'd do if I couldn't find my way out of my delinquent behavior.

My parents had recently found some pornographic pictures in my wallet. I'd torn them from a magazine that Steve had found—geez, did the kid ever lift his head when he walked, or was he forever casting his eyes to what he might find at his feet?—and folded them and hidden them away, or so I thought, in a compartment of my wallet.

I came back from playing sandlot football one afternoon—what need did I have of a wallet on the football field?—and there they were on the dining table. These photos weren't just a bit of risqué cheesecake. They were pictures of women with their legs spread. They were what we called beaver shots.

To see them on display on our dining table with its white tablecloth, its dainty glass candy dish, and my mother's Bible put me to shame. To know that my genteel mother had unfolded these pages, had looked at these women, had known that I'd looked at them too, emptied me of any lame protest I might have been tempted to make. Though my vantage point now tells me those photos were merely part of a typical teenage boy's sexual curiosity, when I filter them through the lens of my mother, who stood at the table, a sad look on her face, I call myself depraved. I call myself corrupt and dissolute. I see myself beyond saving.

My father was angry. "Where did you get these?" He banged his hooks together, turning them so he could pry up the corner of a page and take it between his pincers. He waved it in the air. "I asked you a question. Tell me."

I tried only one defense. "I can't believe you looked in my wallet. It's private."

Even then I knew I had no right to be indignant.

"Don't play like you're the victim," my father said.

Of course, that's exactly what I was doing. Caught at something, I acted like my accusers were the wrongdoers, and I was their prey.

The clock on the wall was ticking. My parents were waiting.

I told them everything. When you're truly caught, there's nothing you can do but tell the truth. That's what I was learning. Then you wait for the consequences.

"You're grounded, Mister," my father said. "One month."

I started to say that wasn't fair, but then my mother said, "If you have something you have to hide, you should know that it's wrong."

What about the fifth of Old Grand-Dad my father kept hidden in the kitchen cabinet? He had it sitting on a board that braced the front of the cabinet between its door and the wall. The bottle was pushed back into a dark corner, so I had to get on my knees and reach my arm back to find it. I wanted to ask about that, but I didn't.

That's when my mother said the thing that stung me the most. "I thought we raised you better than this," she said. "Mercy, what's become of you?"

I should have told her then. I should have said I was lost and didn't know how to save myself. But all I wanted was to be away from those shameful pictures and from the anguished look on my mother's face when she said, "Oh, Lee. My word."

The next day when I was alone in the house after school, I called Amy.

"I want to tell you goodbye." We hadn't been speaking since our breakup, but all the times we had were still painfully fresh in my mind. We'd been close, and it seemed important to me that I tell her what I was going to do.

"I'm leaving," I said. "I'm going to Oak Forest, and I don't intend to come back."

Sure there was a part of me that wanted to hear her respond with concern, to say, no, don't go, to maybe even say she'd miss me, *had* missed me, and hadn't she been stupid to break up with me in the first place. In my heart of hearts, I supposed I wished she'd say she couldn't live without me, and then we'd be back together. I'd forget my plan to run. I'd stay.

But what she said was, "That doesn't seem like a smart thing to do."

Of course, it wasn't a smart thing to do. Part of me knew it even then, but to hear her say it only made me more determined to follow through with my plan.

"I'm going tomorrow night," I said. "Steve and Ricky and me."

Surely now she'd tell me how much I meant to her. Surely, she'd say, *Oh, Lee. Please don't.*

For the longest time, she didn't say anything. I started to wonder whether she'd hung up. I was about to say her name. Then, in a quiet voice I thought sounded distant and cold, she said, "OK."

"OK," she said, and that was that.

The next day, at lunchtime, I went uptown to the bank and withdrew the $200 that I had in my savings account. The teller was a tall, good-natured man—the sort of man you'd imagine had been an Eagle Scout, a Junior Rotarian, a Sons of the American Revolution scholarship award winner. He was a straight arrow, but not in a stick-up-his-ass sort of way. He was a good neighbor, a solid citizen, a man you liked because he liked you.

"What do you plan to do with the money?" he asked me.

He was smiling. He had a little gap between his front teeth, which somehow made him look even more friendly.

"I'm going to buy a car."

"You don't say." I saw him look past me, out the window to where Steve and Ricky were waiting on the sidewalk. "What kind of car do you intend to buy?"

He was getting the money from his cash drawer. I named the first car that came to mind. "A GTO," I told him.

He gave a low whistle. "A GTO," he said. "Now that's a fast car."

"Yes, sir."

"You want to be careful with a car like that."

"I will be, sir."

He looked me straight in the eye, and his voice flattened out for just an instant. "How would you like that money?" he said.

"Twenties would be fine."

"Yes, sir," he said.

I sat in my Spanish class that afternoon, that wad of twenties stuffed down inside the pocket of my jeans. I kept sticking my hand into that pocket just to feel the bulk and to remind myself the money was there.

That's what I did when Mr. Weber appeared in the doorway.

"Mrs. Polston, I'm sorry to interrupt." He bowed slightly to her. Then he straightened and surveyed the room. His gaze finally fell directly on me. "Lee," he said. He crooked his finger and motioned for me to come to him. "Bring your books," he said. "You won't be coming back."

I followed him down the stairs, listening to the wheeze of his breathing. He didn't say a word. I followed him into the office, past the two secretaries at their typewriters, and to the closed door to his private office. He opened the door and stood aside so I could enter.

That's when I saw my mother and father. My mother was twisting a handkerchief in her hands. My father was holding his cap between the pincers of his hook. They were so much older than my friends' parents. They looked old and tired and worn down by time and the indiscretions and misadventures of their son.

Steve and Ricky were there with their mothers. They wouldn't look at me. They just sat there with their heads down.

Mr. Weber said, "It seems like there's mischief afoot."

What a thing to say, I remember thinking at the time, as if what we had here was an honest-to-goodness caper. We were planning to take it on the lam, but Weber had cheesed us.

But of course, it wasn't funny. There wasn't a damned thing funny about it.

Which my father pointed out. "There's not a damned thing funny about this," he said. My lips must have turned up into a grin for just an instant, and of course, he'd seen it. "If you think there is, you've got another think coming, Mister."

That was enough to start everyone else talking.

Ricky's mother said, "They were going to use *my* car." She was a fleshy woman who wore her hair, obviously black with dye, in a beehive. "My Buick," she said.

Steve's mother was a tall, thin woman, who must have been craving a Salem cigarette, the brand she smoked. "Steve, are you doing drugs?" she asked. "Is this what this is all about?"

"No," Steve said.

"What I want to know," my father said, "is whose idea this was."

He was glaring at me, and I knew he expected me to answer. "No one's in particular," I said.

"It was all of our idea," Steve said.

That was too much for me. The thought that he'd protect me when I'd had to persuade him made me wince with guilt.

"No, it wasn't." I decided to come clean. "It was mine."

Ricky's mother threw her hands up in the air. "And he was going to make my son steal my car."

"No one was making me do anything," Ricky said.

But in a way, I was. If I hadn't had the idea—if I hadn't said "I'm leaving"— we wouldn't have been there; we'd all have been going about the regular business of our days.

"Well," said Steve's mother, "I suppose it's like that song says, one bad apple spoils the barrel."

She was talking about the song by the Osmond Brothers, the one that said one bad apple didn't spoil the whole bunch. Steve's mother had misspoke, and it was something we'd laugh about later, as we would Ricky's mother's trauma over the thought that her Buick would have been the getaway car. But we didn't laugh about anything to do with my father and mother, who were obviously the ones most pained by what was happening.

Mr. Weber asked me if I had the money. The bank teller had called him to alert him to the fact that there might be a problem—there might be mischief afoot—and Mr. Weber had called everyone's parents and rounded up the suspects.

I told him I did.

"Give it to your mother, son."

This is the hardest memory, the one of taking that wad of twenties from my pocket and handing them to my mother. She still wouldn't look at me. Everyone watched her straighten the bills. She took great pains to do so. She smoothed each one with her fingers, those fingers that were red and raw from the detergent in the laundry room at the nursing home. She counted the money, and when she was done, she put it inside her pocketbook and kept her head bowed.

There was never anything funny about that, a good woman having to count that money, a sign that her faith in me had been undeserved. I was someone she couldn't trust.

For a while Steve and Ricky and I had to meet with a school psychologist. We didn't mind. It got us out of an afternoon class, and we really didn't talk about anything of much consequence. In fact, I can barely remember what we did talk about. I can barely remember the school psychologist or the few sessions we had with him. I remember he had a black mustache, the kind with long hairs that hung over his upper lip. He had that moustache, and he wore wide neckties with loud patterns and bell-bottomed pants, and we knew he smoked cigarettes because we saw his pack of Marlboros when he opened his briefcase.

The only thing I remember clearly is that we talked about Woodstock and Jimi Hendrix's performance of "The Star-Spangled Banner." The school psychologist was the one who brought it up.

"What do you think of that?" he asked.

He sat on top of the teacher's desk in a vacant classroom, and we sat at three desks in front of him.

"It's all right," Steve said. He fancied himself a rock and roll critic. He went on to say his favorite tracks on the Woodstock album belonged to Canned Heat and Country Joe and the Fish. "Now that's rock music," he said.

"Well, it caused quite a bit of controversy," the school psychologist said. "A lot of people thought it was disrespectful. What do you think about that?"

He was always trying to get us to say what we thought, what we felt.

"It's just a song," Steve said.

"It's our national anthem," said the school psychologist.

We all three snuck looks at one another, smirks on our faces. We weren't stupid. We were just "troubled," and the school psychologist, so he explained to us, was there to help us understand why.

"I believe I heard that somewhere," Steve said. "Maybe in school?"

Ricky and I chuckled.

"Sorry," the school psychologist said. "I didn't mean to imply you were stupid."

"We're not stupid," I said.

And the school psychologist said, "No, you're not. Not at all."

That was our conversation about Woodstock and Jimi Hendrix.

The school psychologist didn't show up for our next session, or the one after that, and no one made mention of our needing to continue, so apparently someone had decided we were no longer in need of counseling.

I remember the feeling of life going on. Though Steve and Ricky and I made fun of the school psychologist for a while and how he'd tried to win our trust by pretending he was one of us, deep down I knew I was in trouble. I knew I wanted to regain my mother's faith. I knew I wanted to be a better son than I'd been.

But there was still the rest of the school year to get through. I continued to shoplift record albums and cigarettes, even after the thrill and pleasure of doing so had gone away. I continued to drink and roam the streets looking for the next thing that would make the time pass and give us something to talk about later. Sometimes we pulled stunts well beneath the maturity level we should have been reaching. One night, we lobbed tomatoes from an alley into a backyard gathering, splattering the guests and leaving us running wildly into the dark when one of them decided to give chase. We ended up crouching behind my house as his car went down our street.

Just a little something like that to get the blood pumping.

Other times, we were more criminal. Steve and Ricky had started to smoke marijuana, and I was hesitant to join them. That decision would be the one that would eventually bring me back to safe ground. For whatever reason, I was afraid to try pot, and I never did, nor have I ever tried any other recreational drug outside of alcohol. As willing as I was to stray from the straight and narrow, I had an ethical line I wouldn't cross.

"C'mon," Steve said, "it's cool."

"It's not for me," I said, and little by little we began to drift apart.

But not before I had one more chance to embarrass myself and my mother as well.

It happened on a Sunday night at our school's baccalaureate service. Steve and Ricky and I drank a few beers before going, just enough to make us tipsy.

We were late arriving. The service had already begun in our school gymnasium. The graduates were gathered, seated on folding chairs set up on the gym floor. They faced the stage where a local minister was giving the benediction. Parents and other relatives were seated on the bleachers, as were friends or just people from our town who took an interest, people like my mother.

I knew she was there, her head bowed, as the minister prayed.

"And bless these young people," he said into the microphone, "that they might live their lives in a way that will be pleasing to you, oh Lord."

We should have stopped and waited until the prayer was done. We never should have pushed open the heavy gym doors and let them come to a shut with a bang behind us. We never should have tried to find a place on the bleachers, our boots clomping, as we stomped up the aisle. We should have had more respect than that.

At one point, Ricky stumbled and nearly fell, and that sent us into a fit of laughter. As the minister went on with the prayer—"And bless them that they should be upright members of their community"—we couldn't stop laughing. *Upright members* had sounded pretty sexual to us, and that made us laugh even more.

I was aware that people around us were lifting their heads and opening their eyes to see exactly who was causing such a disturbance. I knew that somewhere in that gym, my mother was one of them.

Somehow we made it through the service without anyone asking us to leave, and when it was done, we walked the streets a bit more, just goofing around, before we decided to call it a night and head home.

By the time I stepped into my house, my mother had given my father the full report.

"I can't tell you how humiliated I was," she said.

"You must be drunk," my father said. "Are you drunk?"

He was sitting in his reclining chair by the drop leaf table in the dining room. My mother, still in the suit she'd worn to the baccalaureate, was pacing the floor, more upset than I'd ever seen her.

"What?" I said, trying to play innocent. "What did I do?"

That's when my mother stopped pacing. She turned on her heel and pointed her finger at me. Her voice, when she spoke, was sharp. "You know what you did. Don't act like you don't."

I knew then that I was pushing her too far. I was risking any chance I had of regaining her faith in me, but I couldn't keep myself from acting like she was making something out of nothing.

"So we were a little late," I said. "Big deal."

"It's not just that," she said, "and you know exactly what I'm talking about. The whole town was there. The whole town saw what sort of boy you are. The whole town."

Something about the way she kept repeating "the whole town" made me angry, not so much at her but more at myself for having those beers, for showing my ass, for putting her in this position.

"You were drunk," my father said.

And I snapped. "A few beers, that's all. You drink stronger stuff than that."

"What's that supposed to mean?"

I was fully indignant now, an indignation I manufactured in order to portray myself as the victim. "You get drunk," I said, though I'd never seen my father drunk. "And you and Mom go out at night and you don't come back until late, and who knows what goes on while you're gone."

Of course, my parents went visiting some nights while I was alone in the house, but the suggestion that they were carousing was ridiculous.

My father laughed. "He's lost his mind," he said.

That's when I stormed into the kitchen and got the Old Grand-Dad out of the cabinet. I brought it and a juice glass back into the dining room and sat down at the drop leaf table.

"You're not," my father said.

I opened the bottle. "Stop me."

"Beulah, can you believe what you're seeing?"

My mother couldn't answer because now she'd begun to cry. Her father had had a drinking problem before she publicly shamed him by setting the empty whiskey bottles he'd hidden out on their step for anyone passing by to see. I wouldn't know this until years after this night when an aunt would tell me that story, but I did know my uncle was an alcoholic. I'd heard my mother and father talk about his "condition" many times. In short, I knew I was hurting her when I poured a little Old Grand-Dad into my glass.

"Beulah, stop him," my father said. I'd been so brazen I'd rendered him powerless. My mother was weeping.

I downed that whisky.

That's when she said, in a broken voice, husky and raw and quavering with misery, "You want to ruin your life? Well, go on. Just go on, but don't expect me to care."

"All right, then." Now I was crying, too. Crying because I was ashamed, crying because I couldn't seem to keep myself from hurting my mother, crying because I wished I could tell her I was sorry. "All right," I said again. "I won't."

Go

*W*hen you're falling, as I was then, how do you know when you've reached the bottom? You know there has to be one—there has to be an end—but you can find yourself falling again, and you can start to believe the bottom will never come.

I spent the summer still looking for trouble with Steve and Ricky from time to time even though I knew eventually my friendship with them would end. They were spending more and more time with older boys who were providing them with weed and the acid that would eventually ruin Ricky's beautiful mind. I still refused to be a part of that world.

One evening in late summer, one of the last free days before school started, I was walking down the street with Steve and Ricky. We were just hanging out, the way we did, just waiting to see what might come our way, when a car, a two-door Gran Torino, pulled up alongside us. The driver, a criminal boy named JT, hung his arm out the window. He revved the engine and slapped his hand against the door. His shaggy bangs hung down over his eyes.

"C'mon," he said. He said it like a command, and I knew he was talking to Steve and Ricky. "Let's go."

"You got it?" Steve said.

JT put his fingers to his lips and mimed taking a toke off a joint. "*Muy bueno*," he said.

Steve looked at me.

"Ditch him," JT said.

Steve shrugged his shoulders as if to say he didn't know what else to do. "Sorry, man," he said to me, and then he and Ricky got into the car, and JT smoked his tires, and the Gran Torino left black marks on the street. Its brake lights came on for only an instant at the stop sign on the corner, and then it was gone, out into the country. I stood there, alone, listening to the whine of its engine as JT took it through its gears.

I walked the streets awhile, feeling sorry for myself, knowing, I think, that I was close to the end of my friendship with Steve and Ricky. They'd go on to be the kinds of boys that they were going to be, and I'd go on to be the kind that I would be. The only thing was, I still didn't know exactly who that boy was.

Then one Indian summer day at the start of my junior year in high school, I got a glimpse. I'd gone to Wanda's little store on the street over from mine for lunch. Steve and Ricky were there. It was our habit as we got older to go to the store for lunch instead of eating in the school cafeteria—well, at least what we called lunch: Hershey bars, Pepsi-Colas, potato chips, Hostess fruit-filled pies. I hadn't known that Steve and Ricky would be there, and conversation between us was strained. Since the night they'd deserted me for JT and the weed he had for them, I'd kept my distance.

We leaned against the pop case at the front of the store. In all honesty, I have no memory of what we talked about. I only remember the uncomfortable feeling of being in their company. They'd once meant a good deal to me, and now they didn't. They were heading off in a direction I didn't want to go, and talking to them was a little like making conversation with strangers and a little like saying goodbye to the boy I'd been. In our awkward silences, I heard what we couldn't bring ourselves to say—that our friendship was over, that we would have different lives, that I didn't approve of them, that I thought I was somehow superior.

I didn't really think that, but I know to them it must have seemed that I did. Actually, I thought I was lacking somehow. Even now, whenever I listen to my friends talk about their pot-smoking days, and they finally wrangle out of me the truth that I never tried it, not even once, I feel something shift between us. I imagine them thinking, *Who does he think he is?*

The truth is, I know something about myself. I must have sensed it all those years ago even though I couldn't articulate the fact that I was prone to addiction. What I like, I like a lot. My grandfather and my uncle were alcoholics, and my mother worried I'd become one too. I didn't. I learned the art of restraint. I learned to enjoy my pleasures a little at a time. Some I gave up completely because I knew I'd never be able to achieve moderation. Cigarettes, caffeinated coffee, sugary treats.

That day in the store, I was leaving Steve and Ricky behind because I sensed if I went with them, I'd never make my way back. I'd disappear.

"I gotta go," I said.

Next to the pop case was a rack that held boxes of Hostess snack cakes. Wanda was behind the counter, and I was clearly in her line of sight. It was a warm, sunny day, and I had no need of a coat. I had no idea why I picked up a box of Ding Dongs and walked out of the store with them.

Steve and Ricky followed.

"Are you crazy?" Steve said.

Said Ricky, "You know she saw you."

I figured they were right. How could she not have? At the time, I told myself that was why I went back, but now I think it was more than that. Now I think it was my way of coming clean; it was my way of saving myself.

In the store, I walked up to the counter and laid the box of Ding Dongs on it. "I stole these," I said.

Wanda looked at me with such pain on her face. Gray wisps of hair frizzed out from the bun at the back of her head. She was sweating, and her glasses had slipped down on her nose. She was wearing a sleeveless cotton dress, a dingy apron tied around her ample waist. This was a woman who worked so hard for so little, and I'd stolen from her. This was a woman with her own troublesome son, and I'd even stolen from him. They were a family doing the best they could to love each other, and I'd intruded on them. I see now that each time I stole—cigarettes, Hostess Ding Dongs, beer—I wasn't just taking merchandise; I was taking another bit of their privacy.

"I'm sorry," I said.

She pressed her lips together in a tight line. She shook her head. "How could you steal from me?"

I didn't know how to answer. I didn't know how to say I was stupid and young. I didn't know how to say I wanted someone to help me.

So I said, "If you need to call the police, go ahead."

She took a breath and then let it out. A bra strap slid down her arm, and she pulled it into place.

Something about that nearly broke my heart, making plain to me, as it did, how desperately she was trying to hold her life together. And I'd stolen from her. I'd stolen something I didn't even particularly need or want. Something frivolous. Something I could walk into my house and find waiting for me. I could have all the Ding Dongs I wanted, but what I wanted more was to steal for the pure fact of it. Had I been trying to impress Steve and Ricky? Had I been trying to say, I won't smoke weed with you, but I'll still do this? Or was I doing what was necessary in order to bring this all to the end?

In retrospect, I can say this was the bottom. I'd dropped all this way and would drop no more.

"You won't do this again, will you?" Wanda said.

"No, I won't. I surely won't."

She studied me for a good, long while. "You better get back to school," she finally said. "You don't want to be late."

"Yes, ma'am," I said, and I walked out of that store and up the street where Steve and Ricky were waiting for me. All the way back to school, they laughed about how stupid I was to steal that box of Ding Dongs and then have to tuck my tail between my legs and slink back into the store to confess.

I didn't care. We were done.

That was the moment when everything changed for me. I got myself right. I flew straight. I devoted myself to my studies and gradually started to regain a sense of the boy I'd been before I almost left him behind forever, before I came close to getting rid of him.

My English class started a school newspaper, the *Scimitar*. We lived on the northern fringe of a part of the state known as Little Egypt. The name came from the 1800s when one year the corn crop failed in the northern part of the state, and people had to drive their wagons downstate to buy corn the way Joseph's brothers were sent to buy grain in Egypt. We were, though it seems hard to believe now, the Sumner Arabs. I remember the fans at our basketball games singing "We are the Arabs, the mighty, mighty Arabs."

A scimitar is a sword with a curved blade that originated in the Middle East. One might think that our newspaper's objective then would have been hard-hitting journalism, slicing down to the truth. Instead we were a gossip rag with games and puzzles and jokes and student profiles. We came out with a mimeographed issue once a week and sold them for a few cents at lunchtime. I remember one feature called Snoopy Snoops. It was a gossip column. "What was BD doing at JC's house well after midnight?" That sort of thing. Thank goodness I was keeping my nose clean; otherwise, I'd have been skewered weekly.

Sometimes we printed poems and stories and artwork that students wrote. Although I was the sports reporter, I often contributed poems. Our teacher, Mrs. Maynard, was always quick to compliment me. I even started writing a sports column for the local newspaper, the *Sumner Press*, and I contributed an editorial once about the need for a teen center in our town.

All of a sudden, I had opinions, and people actually read what I wrote.

By this time, my algebra teacher, Mr. Miller, the one who'd told me he hoped I'd get myself straightened out, had left to work on a graduate degree at Eastern Illinois University. When our geometry teacher took a few of us to tour the campus during our senior year, we paid Mr. Miller a visit.

"I always read your columns in the *Sumner Press*," he told me. "You really make the games come to life for me."

I could see he was proud, and I felt proud too. Suddenly I had the power of the written word.

One night, close to my graduation, my mother went to an auction at the school and came home with a box of used books.

"I thought you might like some of these," she said, and I knew that I'd gradually won back her faith. This gift was a sign that she believed in me once again.

Stendhal's *The Red and the Black*, Max Shulman's *Rally Round the Flag, Boys!*, Charles Webb's *The Graduate*, Jane Austen's *Pride and Prejudice*, James Leo Herlihy's *Midnight Cowboy*—this was the beginning, or maybe the beginning was further back to the days when I was a small boy and my mother and I sat in Doc Stoll's office, and she opened a *Highlights for Children* and started to read to me, or when she enrolled me in that children's book club and stood up to my father when he tried to put a stop to that, or when she took me to a public library for the first time and taught me to love books.

I don't know what happened to most of the books from that box over the years, but I'll wager I let most of them go at the auction I had after both my parents were gone. Those last two books, though, are still on my shelves. I can take them down and press them to my nose and breathe in their musty scent and find myself transported back to our house and its hardwood floors and its wraparound porch and its small kitchen where we gathered each day for our meals.

My mother kept a radio on the counter, and mornings I'd wake to the sound of a State Farm jingle: "And like a good neighbor, State Farm is there." I'd force myself to rise, and if it were winter, I'd stand in front of the gas heating stove in our dining room, letting the hot air warm me. Then I'd go on to the kitchen where my mother would have my breakfast waiting.

How many meals she must have cooked. I remember after my father died, and she lived alone, she'd cook such small portions for herself. I lived nearly two hours away from her at that time, and sometimes I'd find myself thinking about her sitting at that chrome dinette set where once my father and I had sat with her, letting the radio play just for the company it provided.

I think about them and their last minutes together. My father said he was going out to mow the yard despite the summer heat.

"I've almost got supper ready," my mother said to him, trying to convince him to stay inside.

"I'll just do a little bit," he told her and went out to mow.

She was at the stove when, a few minutes later, she heard the lawnmower's throttle rev and stick, its loud noise a howl to the heavens. She looked out the window and saw my father's body on the grass.

At that moment, I was in my apartment in Evansville, Indiana, packing for a move to Fayetteville, Arkansas. I'd been accepted into their MFA program. I'd graduated with my BA and MA in English from Eastern Illinois University, and I'd dedicated three years to writing short stories while working full time.

By this time, my father and I had reconciled. We'd come out the other side of our anger and found we were able to love each other. He'd even clipped a column I did for the *Evansville Courier,* in which I'd written about him on Father's Day, and carried it uptown to Tubby's Barber Shop to show to the loafers there.

"Your father was proud of you," my mother told me. "He was very proud."

He was content, there toward what none of us knew were the last days of his life, to tend to his garden and his fruit trees. A first heart attack had convinced him to give up the farming he loved so much and to lease his ground. He'd thrown himself into his recovery the way he did everything in his life—with force. He bought an exercise bicycle and set out to lose weight. He walked when the weather permitted; at other times, he rode his bike. He rode it so vigorously that I worried about him. He rode it until he was sweating and panting for breath. He lost weight. He tried to watch his diet. His heart disease was one more challenge he meant to meet. He was stubborn that way, and he'd passed that willfulness on to me. It's been with me through every disappointment in my writing life. In many ways, my father was as tempered as the steel of his hooks, and though it often led him into situations that embarrassed us all, it also allowed him to go on with his life. He gave his determination and fire to me. It was his greatest gift, just as my mother's compassion was hers.

The summer he died, he liked to invite me to come out to the garden with him in the evenings once the temperatures had cooled. He liked to check on his plants and to tell me to pick a bit of this and that to take home with me.

He was particularly proud of his peach trees, the ones he'd planted in our backyard when we'd first moved in. They were mature now. They were producing peaches.

"Pick that one," he told me, one evening a few weeks before he died. I did as he asked. I snapped off the peach and felt its fuzz on my fingers. I smelled its aroma. I held it to my father's nose so he could smell it too. "Let's have a bite," he said. I held the peach so he could bite into it. Juice dribbled onto his chin, and he used his sleeve to wipe it away. "Now you," he said.

"I like mine peeled," I told him.

"One bite," he said.

Dusk was upon us. The cicadas were chirring, and a breeze moved through the leaves of the peach trees. If anyone were to have looked out onto our yard at that moment, they would have barely been able to see us. They would have only known that two people stood there in the almost dark. They would have had no idea how we'd fought, how we'd suffered, how we finally learned to love without injury. They certainly wouldn't have known that twenty-six years ago in Doc Stoll's office, my father had tried to prevent my birth. I didn't even know it at that point. I only knew my father wanted me to take a bite from that peach, a peach he'd grown. It was important to him, and I did it. I bit into the peach and tasted its sweetness and let the juice dribble down my chin.

That communion. That's the last memory I want to have of my father.

"Let's go in," he said, and we did.

But there's one memory more. The last time I saw him alive. He and my mother had come to Evansville for a doctor's appointment. She was suffering the TIAs that would eventually lead to her dementia. I took a photograph of them. My father was sitting at the dining table, his tweed hat on, ready to get on the road for home; my mother was standing behind him in a green dress with white polka dots, the corners of her lips lifting up into a slight grin.

When I look at that photograph now, I note that my father looks tired. He's worn out with worry—worry over my mother's health, worry over what might happen to him should her health fail further. At this point, he also knows I'm moving ten hours away to Arkansas. After his death, an old high school classmate of his will tell me something my father said that in retrospect will be eerie. He was telling his old classmate about me going to Arkansas.

"My job's done with him now," my father said. "I guess I can rest."

When I walked my parents out to their car, I told my father not to work too hard. He assured me he wouldn't. Those were the last words we'd ever say to each other. After so many words—and so many of them said in anger—those were the last.

"Don't work too hard," I said.

And he said, "I won't."

I was twenty-six years old when I said goodbye to my father, and I was two weeks away from leaving my mother. I almost stayed. I sat at the kitchen table with her the night of my father's visitation, and I said, "I won't go."

"Your father would want you to," she said without hesitation, even though she must have known the lonely days she was about to encounter. "Your father was a fighter," she said. "Go after your dreams. He taught you that."

And it was true; he had.

"But you—"

She wouldn't let me finish. "I'll be fine," she said.

The night I left, intending to drive through the darkness to St. Louis and then down into the Ozarks, I told her goodbye.

"Be careful," she said.

I was already close to tears. Something was ending—I knew that—and something exciting was about to begin. I was both frightened and thrilled. I was having my chance to have the life I'd always wanted. I wanted to write and to teach, but to do that I would have to leave my newly widowed mother behind. In many ways, I was still the shy boy who'd once clung to her skirts, afraid to show my face to the world, but I was also a fatherless son now, ready to make my own way.

"Mom," I said.

We were standing on the porch in the glow of the dining room light coming through the screen door. My mother's back was stooped as if all the years she'd spent with my father were pressing down on her, both his presence and now his absence. Or as if the pain I'd helped cause was pulling her toward the ground. Still she managed a shy grin—always that sweet, shy grin, the look of a woman who had faith that everything would be all right. I wanted to say so much more to her. I wanted to thank her for the love she'd given me, for all the times she'd read to me when I was young, for inviting me to know the world through language and story, for all her faith in me even when I didn't deserve it, for letting me go.

"Let me know that you get there all right," she said.

"I will," I told her, and then I got in the car and pulled out onto the street.

She was still standing on the porch waving at me. I had miles and miles to go and years and years to live. Although I didn't know it then—could only hope and dream—there would be books for me to write, stories for me to tell, countless students to teach. All I knew that night was that I would have a chance. My father's fire and my mother's encouragement were giving it to me. All the way up the street, I kept glancing in my rearview mirror. She was still there, watching my taillights as I drove away from her.

How could she have known, all those years ago when she picked up a *Highlights for Children* magazine in Doc Stoll's waiting room and began to read to me, that eventually—it must have seemed like it happened in a blink of an eye—this day would come?

At the end of our block, I turned left. There was nothing now but the empty streets of the town, the lights on in store fronts on the main street, and then the businesses dwindling as I made my way to the highway, the hard road that would take me out of town, to the flat prairie land where out across the fields pole lights would be on in barnyards, to the steady click of my tires over the seams in the road, each mile taking me closer, and still closer, to where my mother wanted me to go.

If I close my eyes, I can still see her on that porch in the dim light, her hand raised as if to bless me, as if to say, *Go on. Go. Go have the life I gave you.*

Lee Martin is author of the novels *The Bright Forever*, a finalist for the 2006 Pulitzer Prize for Fiction; *River of Heaven*; *Quakertown*; *Break the Skin*; *Late One Night*; and *Yours, Jean*. His memoirs are *From Our House*, *Turning Bones*, and *Such a Life*. He is also author of two short story collections, *The Least You Need To Know* and *The Mutual UFO Network*. He is coeditor of *Passing the Word: Writers on Their Mentors* and author of a craft book, *Telling Stories: The Craft of Narrative and the Writing Life*. His fiction and nonfiction have appeared in such places as *Harper's Magazine*, *Ms.*, *Creative Nonfiction*, the *Georgia Review*, the *Kenyon Review*, *Fourth Genre*, *River Teeth*, the *Southern Review*, *Prairie Schooner*, *Glimmer Train*, *The Best American Essays*, and *The Best American Mystery Stories*. He is winner of the Mary McCarthy Prize in Short Fiction and recipient of fellowships from the National Endowment for the Arts and the Ohio Arts Council. He teaches in the MFA Program at The Ohio State University, where he is a College of Arts and Sciences Distinguished Professor and where he was also winner of the 2006 Alumni Award for Distinguished Teaching.